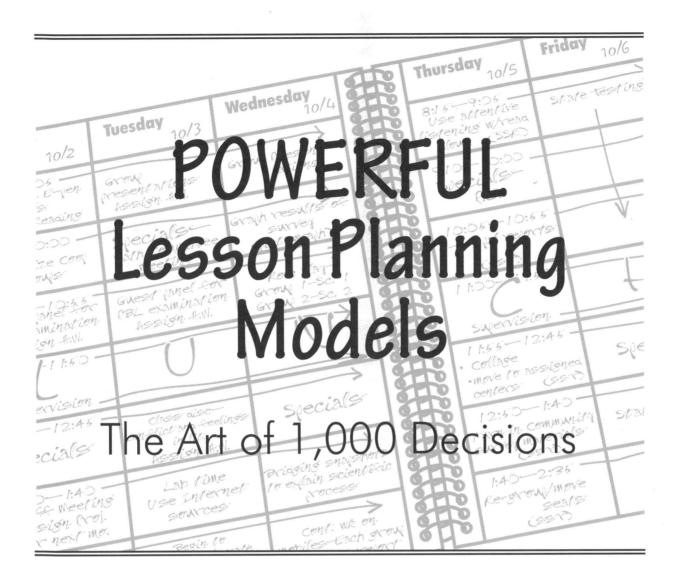

POWERFUL
Lesson Planning Models

The Art of 1,000 Decisions

Janice Skowron

Arrendale Library/Piedmont College

Foreword by
Charlotte Danielson

SkyLight
Professional
Development

Arlington Heights, Illinois

D1318542

Powerful Lesson Planning Models

Published by SkyLight Professional Development
2626 S. Clearbrook Dr., Arlington Heights, IL 60005
800-348-4474 or 847-290-6600
Fax 847-290-6609
info@skylightedu.com
http://www.skylightedu.com

LCCCN 00-107342
ISBN 1-57517-349-2

2777-McN
Item Number 2134
Z Y X W V U T S R Q P O N M L K J I H G F E D C
08 07 06 05 04 03 02   15 14 13 12 11 10 9 8 7 6 5 4 3

There are
one-story intellects,
two-story intellects, and
three-story intellects with skylights.

All fact collectors, who have no aim beyond their facts, are

one-story minds.

Two-story minds
compare, reason, generalize,
using the labors of the fact collectors
as well as their own.

Three-story minds
idealize, imagine, predict—their best illumination
comes from above,

through the **skylight**.

—Oliver Wendell Holmes

Dedication

To Raymond—for his support, enthusiasm, advice, and friendly criticism.

Contents

Foreword

DESIGNING INSTRUCTION

Powerful Lesson Planning Models is an important book, offering teachers essential guidance in the highly complex task of lesson planning. It provides four models: basic, integrated, differentiated, and problem-based. These models are progressively complex and nuanced, providing teachers with guidance as they increase their lesson planning proficiency.

As I set forth in *Enhancing Professional Practice: A Framework for Teaching,* planning is one of the four essential domains of professional practice (Danielson 1996). Further, planning is, of course, highly cerebral, requiring high-level thinking and decision-making. And in this age of content standards and the high-stakes assessments of those standards, the teacher's challenge in planning for instruction is more profound then ever.

Textbooks and other instructional materials provide teachers with learning objectives, activities, assessments, and of course, materials needed—all they need for instructional planning. Teachers have the option, if they so choose, to simply follow the directions, and "connect the dots." In many cases, the instructional suggestions offered by the textbooks and ancillary materials are as viable as those that many teachers (particularly novices) could create on their own. However, only teachers know their own students (and therefore how to differentiate instruction to assist them), and content standards are different in different locations. Therefore, if teachers can acquire sophisticated planning skills, they will be able to offer a richer instructional environment for their students than if they relied solely on their text materials.

Powerful Lesson Planning Models works equally well for novice teachers and for seasoned professionals. The beginner will likely feel most comfortable with the basic model. With enough practice this model becomes perfected to the extent that it can be built upon. The models described subsequently (integrated, differentiated, and problem-based) are advanced, requiring skills rarely demonstrated by those just entering the profession. The skills and practice needed to successfully implement these models is highly advanced, reflecting a sophisticated level of planning.

Therefore, by mastering the ideas presented in *Powerful Lesson Planning Models,* teachers can advance their practice, and demonstrate skills I have identified as "proficient" and "distinguished" (Danielson 1996). And if teachers can develop these skills in collaboration with their colleagues, their professional experience will be doubly rewarding.

Charlotte Danielson
Lead Developer
Educational Testing Service,
Princeton, NJ

Preface

Do you remember your first teaching assignment—the first day you entered your new classroom and thought about the students who would soon be there? For me it was a combination of pride and anxiety. I was proud that I had finally attained what I had prepared for over the last several years. I was also extremely anxious about the first day with my students. What would they be like? Would they like me? And most important, how could I best teach them? Sure I had been in classrooms before. I had planned and taught lessons. But this was different. This was no short-term assignment with someone to guide me along the way. I was on my own. I had signed the contract, and I was expected to be a professional.

The first few days of my teaching assignment, I was overwhelmed with information about school rules and regulations, extracurricular assignments, curriculum requirements, and schedules. A kindly colleague offered the advice to "always have something for them to do." So I studied all the curriculum guides and teachers' manuals (I had never seen them before!). I made sure I had enough worksheets. I decorated my classroom with bulletin boards and attractive displays. I worked from dawn to midnight for weeks to get ready for the first day. When it arrived, I was exhausted. Somehow my students and I survived that day—I'm sure I learned more than they did. What I learned was that I needed a plan. If I was going to be any good at all at this teaching thing (and I desperately wanted to be), I was the one who had to make it happen. Certainly I could make sure I always had something for them to do, but I wanted to make sure I always had something for them to learn.

Preface

It is interesting the way competence and confidence go hand in hand. After several years, I felt more competent and at ease—but I was still very much a beginning teacher. As I came to know more about how learning happens, I tried different instructional designs. I put several objectives into the same lesson, I tailored lessons for different students, I let students take the lead not only in what they learned but how they learned. There were successes, but there were also disappointments. Not everything worked. But my teaching evolved and my students progressed.

Looking back over my early teaching years, I wish I had had more guidance. I read professional journals and learned a great deal about theory and philosophy, what to do and what not to do. But there was very little on how to actually do it. I wish there had been some models I could have used rather than trying to reinvent the wheel; it would have made teaching easier. I did not realize it then, but this is where the ideas for *Powerful Lesson Planning Models* took root.

Over the years, I have played many roles in education—classroom teacher, reading specialist, administrator, college professor, and consultant. As I listen to and talk with classroom teachers, from kindergarten through high school and in graduate programs and school districts throughout the country, I am taken back to my early experiences as a classroom teacher. I listen as teachers express their concerns and frustrations as well as their joys and desires about teaching. In very candid moments, when expressions of doubt sometimes surface, teachers question their practices. Many realize that the approaches they have used for many years no longer work as well as they once did. Their students have changed—and they have changed. Many are willing to try new approaches but simply don't know how to go about it. So, for lack of information, they go on doing what they've always done. As one veteran teacher said: "This year we're supposed to integrate learning. We had a big meeting where we heard why it's a good idea. But no one told us how to do it. We're left on our own."

Not surprisingly, even experienced teachers who are familiar with basic instructional design may find it difficult to implement more complex instructional approaches. The planning procedures for different approaches involve asking different questions and making different decisions. Experienced teachers, regardless of content area or grade level, need models as they plan more complex instructional designs. Models provide a focus and common language for discussion and understanding.

Learning to plan effective lessons is part of the preparatory coursework in teacher education programs. Preclinical and student teaching experiences provide opportunities for the preservice teacher to observe and discuss lesson plans with experienced practitioners. Initially, preservice and beginning teachers focus on a very basic form of lesson planning that includes defining the learning standards to be achieved, selecting the activities to facilitate learning to meet the standard, and developing an appropriate assessment of student learning. At this stage, practicing more complex planning for diverse classrooms is not the norm (Tomlinson et al. 1997). Unless basic instructional design is understood and practiced, there can be little understanding of how to plan more complex instructional designs. With proficiency in basic instructional design, the beginning teacher is ready to expand and refine his or her teaching. Without this proficiency, the beginning teacher is likely to be confused and bewildered when trying to design something more complex.

Linda Darling-Hammond (1997) tells us that in 2005, over half the teachers in American classrooms will have been hired in the preceding decade. Many students will be taught by novice teachers and others who have come to teaching through alternate paths. Individuals who have content expertise do not always have the pedagogical expertise to design effective instruction. Their effectiveness depends on their ability to analyze content information, skills, and processes in terms of how to teach. An instructional design planning guide provides a tool for these teachers to connect content to instruction.

This book is for those of you who are at the beginning of your teaching career path and for those who desire to make better classrooms for your students through thoughtful planning. It is what I would have wanted those

Preface

many years ago when I first stepped into a classroom. This jump-start of a book makes no assumptions of prior knowledge. It covers the basics of lesson planning, integrated instruction, differentiated instruction, and problem-based learning. Specific examples of planning guides for these approaches serve as models for teachers to form and fit their own ideas into new ways of teaching.

Introduction

An instructional plan sets the stage for teaching and learning. It is the blueprint for instruction. The plan documents what and how students will learn. The purpose of *Powerful Lesson Planning Models* is to bring into focus the multitude of decisions teachers face as they plan instruction. Teachers are guided through four major instructional designs: Basic, Integrated, Differentiated, and Problem-Based.

Instructional design is a thinking process that results in a product—the instructional plan. Powerful Lesson Planning Models provides a series of key questions and a step-by-step process for developing instructional plans. The instructional plan emerges as the teacher contemplates key questions and makes decisions related to them. This structured step-by-step process is used as a starting point. Modifications to fit individual circumstances may be made once the process is fully understood. Descriptive information and instructional design tools—key questions, outlines, templates, and examples—are provided to facilitate the planning process.

OVERVIEW OF THE INSTRUCTIONAL DESIGN PROCESS

Powerful Lesson Planning Models provides Instructional Design Planning Guides comprised of key questions for planning each of the four instructional designs. Each Instructional Design Planning Guide includes three sections: (1) Desired Results, (2) Lesson Design, and (3) Evidence of Learning. The planning process begins with the teacher focusing on the key questions and making decisions related to what students will learn and how that learning will occur. This process produces the "data" the teacher uses to construct more specific learning plans. While the process of using the Instructional Design Planning Guide and completing the Instructional Design form is generally the same for each of the four models, the key questions differ and planning tools are specific to each particular model (see Figure 0.1).

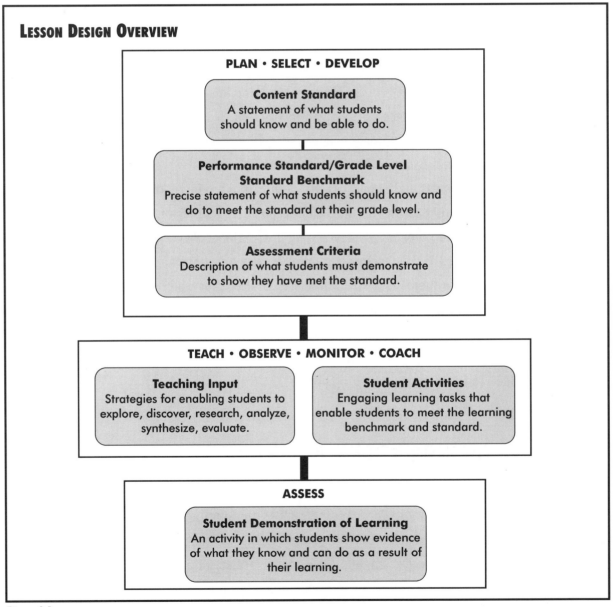

LESSON DESIGN OVERVIEW

PLAN · SELECT · DEVELOP

Content Standard
A statement of what students should know and be able to do.

Performance Standard/Grade Level Standard Benchmark
Precise statement of what students should know and do to meet the standard at their grade level.

Assessment Criteria
Description of what students must demonstrate to show they have met the standard.

TEACH · OBSERVE · MONITOR · COACH

Teaching Input
Strategies for enabling students to explore, discover, research, analyze, synthesize, evaluate.

Student Activities
Engaging learning tasks that enable students to meet the learning benchmark and standard.

ASSESS

Student Demonstration of Learning
An activity in which students show evidence of what they know and can do as a result of their learning.

Figure 0.1

Common to all the instructional plans is the lesson plan that documents the learning standards, assessments, teaching strategies, and learning activities. When teachers practice and perfect using this Basic tool, they are able to design more complex approaches to learning.

Powerful Lesson Planning Models is divided into chapters that cover each instructional model: Basic, Integrated, Differentiated, and Problem-Based. A brief description of each chapter is provided below.

CHAPTER 1: BASIC INSTRUCTIONAL DESIGN

This chapter begins with a discussion of the importance of planning as it relates to expert teaching. The development of intuitive teaching is explained as the result of the teacher's learning, experience, practice, and reflection.

A basic planning structure for teaching specific learning standards is described in chapter one. While learning standards may differ somewhat from state to state, the design process presented in this chapter may be used in any standards-led system. The planning process is made clear through the use of planning templates, models, illustrations, and graphics.

This Basic instructional design model is intended for use by preservice and novice teachers to gain experience in lesson planning. The tools used to develop a Basic lesson plan are summarized below.

1. The Basic Instructional Design Planning Guide with suggested planning resources, notes, and comments. This is meant to assist the teacher in responding to the guiding questions and completing the Basic Instructional Design Plan.
2. The Basic Instructional Design Plan blank form to be completed by the teacher as a planning worksheet.
3. An example of a completed Basic Instructional Design Plan.
4. Lesson Plan Form.

CHAPTER 2: INTEGRATED INSTRUCTIONAL DESIGN

Integrating learning standards from various content areas in meaningful ways for students is the focus of chapter two. It begins with the rationale and research that support integrated learning. The Integrated Instructional Design Planning Guide is provided to facilitate the planning process. The tools used to develop an Integrated Instructional Design Plan are summarized below.

1. The Integrated Instructional Design Planning Guide with suggested planning resources, notes, and comments. This is meant to assist the teacher in responding to the guiding questions and completing the Integrated Instructional Design Plan.
2. The Integrated Instructional Design Plan blank form to be completed by the teacher as a planning worksheet.
3. An example of a completed Integrated Instructional Design Plan.
4. Curriculum Calendar Map.
5. Integrated Instructional Planner—Part 1, Part 2.

The Integrated Instructional Design Plan includes the development of a Curriculum Calendar Map—an overview of the topics/concepts studied in each of the curriculum areas. These topics are translated into learning standards on the Integrated Instructional Planner Part 1 under a major learning theme or "big idea." A teaching overview plan based on the learning standards is developed using the Integrated Instructional Planner Part 2. Specific lesson plans for classroom implementation are developed from this overview.

The instructional design produced in this manner may incorporate many learning standards across the curriculum or focus on a limited number. Planning templates and models are provided throughout the chapter along with illustrations and graphics to make the planning process manageable and user friendly.

CHAPTER 3: DIFFERENTIATED INSTRUCTIONAL DESIGN

Explaining how to accommodate and provide successful learning experiences for students of varying levels of abilities, backgrounds, and learning preferences is the purpose of chapter three. The theory, research, and best practices information associated with differentiation are discussed. This chapter enables teachers to understand why it is important to differentiate instruction and how to go about doing so.

The differentiated instructional design model differentiates learning activities but holds learning standards constant. The basis for differentiation is determined according to student needs and task demands. The tools used to develop a differentiated instructional design are summarized below.

1. The Differentiated Instructional Design Planning Guide with suggested planning resources, notes, and comments. This is meant to assist the teacher in responding to the guiding questions and completing the Differentiated Instructional Design Plan.

2. The Differentiated Instructional Design Plan blank form to be completed by the teacher as a planning worksheet.

3. An example of a completed Differentiated Instructional Design Plan.

4. Differentiated Instructional Design Matrix.

The Differentiated Instructional Design Plan form is used as a planning document. The information produced from this form is used to develop a matrix showing the criteria for student differentiation in relation to the learning standards to be taught. Corresponding instructional activities are then developed for each cell in the matrix. Separate mini-lessons may be developed from this matrix depending on the needs of the students.

CHAPTER 4: PROBLEM-BASED LEARNING INSTRUCTIONAL DESIGN

Problem-based learning is organized around a real-life problem where students take the lead in determining how to go about solving the problem and working though to a resolution. The teacher is a facilitator in the process—offering resources, coaching, monitoring, and conducting mini-lessons. Chapter 4 is an introductory, straightforward explanation of problem-based learning—how it originated, how to develop problem statements, and how to incorporate standards and assessment into problem-based activities. A discussion of the teacher's role in problem-based learning is provided to illustrate the planning perspective required in this approach. The importance and use of technology resources are discussed and sample Web sites are provided.

Problem-based learning appears complex, but teachers may use a variety of planning strategies to make this approach manageable. The thinking process questions provided in chapter four help teachers sort out and see the total picture, even if the details must be filled in later. It is recommended that this instructional design be undertaken after the teacher has had some experience with integrated and differentiated instructional designs.

The tools used to develop a Problem-Based Instructional Design are summarized below.

1. The Problem-Based Learning Instructional Design Planning Guide with suggested planning resources, notes, and comments. This is meant to assist the teacher in responding to the guiding questions and completing the Problem-Based Instructional Design Plan.

2. The Problem-Based Instructional Design Plan blank form to be completed by the teacher as a planning worksheet.

3. An example of a completed Problem-Based Instructional Design Plan.

4. Problem-Based Learning Standards Overview.

5. Problem-Based Learning Assessment Planner.

HOW TO USE THIS BOOK

Preservice and novice teachers will find it helpful to become thoroughly familiar with Basic lesson design as presented in chapter one. A firm grounding in the Basics helps to ensure success in using more complex models. After teachers become confident in planning Basic instruction, they may mentally review or modify the Basic Instructional Design Planning Guide. It is probably not necessary to write out responses to the key questions once the planning process is well known.

Even experienced teachers benefit from having a structure to guide instructional planning. However, the planning process for these teachers is somewhat different, in that their background knowledge enables them to take some shortcuts and make some modifications. Flexibility is built into the planning templates to accommodate a wide range of teaching experience. Experienced teachers may wish to review the Instructional Design Planning Guide to refresh information they already have and tap into their prior knowledge related to instructional planning.

Teachers who have used a single content approach to planning and teaching and are ready to try integrated, differentiated, or problem-based instructional designs benefit from going through the entire thinking process using the Instructional Design Planning Guides. This facilitates in-depth understanding and makes subsequent planning more efficient. It is hoped that *Powerful Lesson Planning Models* will help teachers to revitalize current practices, expand their repertoire of approaches, and improve learning for students.

Basic Instructional Design

Chapter 1 Overview

▶ Harnessing the power of intuitive teaching

▶ Planning that sets the stage for exceptional teaching

▶ Using state standards as a springboard for instructional design

▶ Planning for brain-compatible learning

Basic Instructional Design

It is not difficult to recognize classrooms that are alive with purposeful activity and exude a feeling that "there's important work going on here." Students are engaged in their work. They understand the direction and importance of their activity. The teacher is a facilitator—coaching, questioning, and providing resources for students at opportune times. There is an atmosphere of authenticity that resembles real life. Independence is balanced with interdependence as a means to learning. Some of the time, students learn with others in small groups, some of the time they work independently, and other times they are part of whole class activity. Such a classroom does not just happen. It is the result of careful and precise planning by the teacher.

The difference is in the details . . .

By the same token, it is not difficult to recognize classrooms where learning has little direction or focus. Students are off task and lack a sense of purpose. They appear to be disinterested and bored with activities that hold little challenge. They neither understand the purpose of their work nor believe in its importance. Though the teacher may have good intentions, he or she has not created the foundation necessary for effective learning. There is little evidence of careful and precise planning for instruction.

A critical difference between these classrooms is the underlying plan that details what students will learn and how they will learn it. A well-functioning classroom is based on a well-designed plan. According to Costa and Garmston (1994, 90), "Planning may well include the most important decisions teachers make because it is the phase upon which all other decisions rest." Good planning sets the stage for good teaching, which in turn fosters optimal learning. Teachers who know how to plan know precisely what they want to accomplish—or more exactly, what they want their students to accomplish. Poor planning results in no one, including the teacher, having a clear understanding of what is to be accomplished. Effective instruction starts with an organized instructional plan.

FROM HERE TO INTUITIVE TEACHING

Some teachers appear to be intuitive. They facilitate student learning with ease and agility. They are confident, insightful, and expert. They not only know the standards that constitute accomplished teaching but also are able to translate the standards into practice. Becoming an exceptional teacher is a learning process that some believe never ends. The teacher is in a continual state of learning, building, and refining teaching practices. This complex nature of exceptional teaching is illustrated in Figure 1.1. The outermost layer represents expert teaching actions and behaviors. It is where ease and competence are exhibited—where actions appear to be intuitive. It is easy to observe the effortless actions of teaching in the intuitive layer, but there is

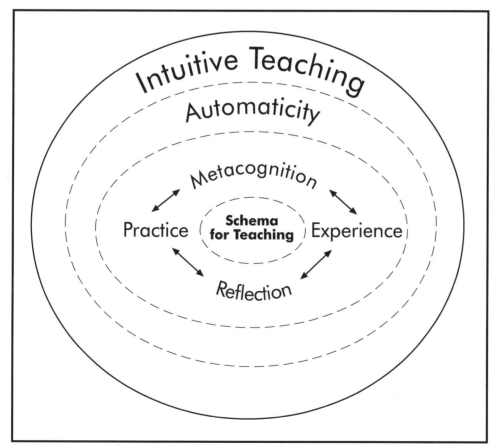

Figure 1.1

much more than meets the eye. Other layers, hidden from view, are powerful determiners of the outer layer.

At the core of the illustration in Figure 1.1 is the teacher's mental schema for teaching. It is an amalgam of all the information, concepts, skills, processes, attitudes, values, and beliefs the teacher holds regarding teaching. The second layer shows the interaction of metacognition, reflection, practice, and experience. This interaction impacts and changes the schema. The third layer is automaticity. Automaticity is a behavior that develops through a multitude of repetitions, knowing how to do something and then engaging in repetitive practice. Such behaviors may be mental or physical (Samuels 1994). Learning to drive a car is an example of automaticity. The inexperienced driver consciously refers to mental notes regarding the physical act of turning the steering wheel and coordinating this with gas pedal pressure, all the while visually judging distance to remain in the appropriate lane and not impact the vehicle directly ahead. The experienced driver, on the other hand, turns the vehicle with effortless ease—with no apparent conscious thought given to the task. Driving the car has become automatic.

The outermost layer is intuitive teaching—the quick, effortless, competent action (automaticity) observed in exceptional teachers. Developing this outer layer is a complex process that happens over time and is unique to every individual.

Now, imagine the two-dimensional image in Figure 1.1 as a three-dimensional sphere made of clear plastic. Imagine the layers within the sphere separated by permeable membranes through which thoughts, ideas, learning, attitudes, beliefs, skills, and knowledge flow freely. Imagine that only the outermost layer of the sphere is observable to others. Those who observe the sphere see only the expert in action. Those who understand the complexity of teaching understand the knowledge, skills, processes, and multitude of experiences that shape the outermost layer.

> Automaticity is a behavior that develops through a multitude of repetitions.

Experience and Practice

Experience is the heart of know-how, as in the expression: "He has real know-how." Know-how does not just happen. It develops through experience and exposure to new ideas, methods, and strategies. It develops as the teacher thinks and reflects on the meaning of the experiences and fits new information into his or her pattern of knowledge. "Professional knowledge is seen as coming both from sources outside the teacher and from the teachers' own interpretations of their everyday experiences" (Sparks-Langer and Colton 1991, 37). Obviously, without exposure to new ideas and ways of doing things, teachers will continue for better or worse with their present practices.

The opportunity to learn new things is critical if teachers are to grow professionally. Professional development programs are one source of knowledge input. But not all things "learned" through professional development will be retained or used. Knowledge must be transferred and applied in real teaching situations. According to Bellanca (1995), effective professional development experiences are consistent with constructivist theory: "Constructivist theoreticians view learning transfer as the most complex and important element in the learning process. Without transfer either by hugging (an immediate connection within the curriculum) or bridging (a wider connection across the curriculum or into life), learning is incomplete. Thus, transfer cannot be an instructional afterthought or something that just 'happens.' It must be a consciously planned result of taking something (a skill, idea, concept, value, etc.) and moving it somewhere (across a lesson, unit, course, job, etc.) by means of a carefully selected somehow" (Bellanca 1995, 18).

Effective teachers plan precisely and comprehensively. They have a clear picture of what they wish to accomplish and how they will go about doing so. They practice the elements of planning and teaching over and over, eventually reaching a point where the elements and actions are internalized, allowing greater ease of use. But practice alone does not ensure improvement. New learning (input) combined with metacognition and reflection contribute to effective practice.

> Effective teachers plan precisely and comprehensively.

Basic Instructional Design

When teachers plan instruction, they engage in a complex mental process. In the beginning, the process is conscious and deliberate. The novice teacher applies a great deal of thought to planning instruction. Every component, every step of the instructional plan is thought through and written out in detail. The teacher visualizes the enactment of the plan, makes changes, refines and completes the plan. The experienced teacher, on the other hand, who has used the instructional design components in planning and teaching, has a well-developed schema for instructional planning. He or she plans easily and efficiently and no longer needs to attend to every precise detail. This teacher has reached a level of "knowing" the answers to myriad of questions and decisions that accompany instructional planning. Deliberate thought is replaced by automatic action (Sparks-Langer and Colton 1991). Instructional planning has reached a level of automaticity that resembles intuition. However, when questioned regarding the purposes, standards, connections, and approaches used, the accomplished teacher is able to fully explain the various lesson elements.

So, is there such a thing as intuitive teaching? Yes—and no. No if the definition of intuitive is instinctive. Yes, in terms of the development of automatic processes. Intuitive teachers are expert planners who understand instructional planning and know how to design instruction. "Intuition" develops through automaticity as teachers use prior knowledge, engage in precision planning, put plans into action, and reflect on the outcome of their instruction.

PROFESSIONAL TEACHING STANDARDS

Danielson's *Enhancing Professional Practice: Framework for Teaching* (1996) describes twenty-two components of teaching divided into four major domains: planning and preparation, classroom environment, instruction, and professional responsibilities. According to Danielson, this framework provides a road map for novice teachers and guidance for experienced teachers.

Further, it may be used as a structure for focusing improvement efforts through professional conversation. And it communicates to the general public the competencies inherent in teaching.

As one delves into the planning and preparation components in the first domain of Danielson's framework, the multifaceted nature of instructional planning becomes more apparent (Figure 1.2). We can see that the teacher's knowledge and understanding of content (a necessary prerequisite) is by itself not sufficient for effective teaching. Likewise the knowledge and understanding of students is not in itself sufficient for effective teaching. Other components—learning objectives, material resources, instructional strategies, and assessment—are woven into an organized and coherent plan of instruction. Like pieces of a puzzle, all components are necessary to achieve the complete picture.

Like Danielson's domains of teaching, professional standards define teaching for a wide range of audiences within and outside the educational profession. Standards document what effective teachers should know and be able to do and provide a common language with in which to discuss professional teaching.

COMPONENTS OF A PROFESSIONAL PRACTICE

DOMAIN 1: PLANNING AND PREPARATION

Demonstrating Knowledge of Content and Pedagogy
 Knowledge of content
 Knowledge of prerequisite relationships
 Knowledge of content-related pedagogy

Demonstrating Knowledge of Students
 Knowledge of characteristics of age group
 Knowledge of students' varied approaches to learning
 Knowledge of students' skills and knowledge
 Knowledge of students' interests and cultural heritage

Selecting Instructional Goals
 Value
 Clarity
 Suitability for diverse students
 Balance

Demonstrating Knowledge of Resources
 Resources for teaching
 Resources for students

Designing Coherent Instruction
 Learning activities
 Instructional materials and resources
 Instructional groups
 Lesson and unit structure

Assessing Student Learning
 Congruence with instructional goals
 Criteria and standards
 Use for planning

Reprinted from *Enhancing Professional Practice: A Framework for Teaching* by Charlotte Danielson. © 1996 by Charlotte Danielson. Reprinted by permission of the author.

Figure 1.2

Basic Instructional Design

STUDENT LEARNING STANDARDS

Just as professional teaching standards define teaching practices, learning standards define what students will know and be able to do. Over fifty years ago, Ralph Tyler (1949, 45) wrote, "The purpose of a statement of objectives is to indicate the kinds of changes in the student to be brought about so that the instructional activities can be planned and developed in a way likely to attain these objectives; that is, to bring about these changes in students." Tyler's description of learning objectives remains useful in planning instruction based on what students should know and be able to do. Today's terminology of standards and benchmarks may differ from Tyler's terms of goals and objectives, but his fundamental ideas still hold true. Today most states have developed content learning standards that are meant to give direction in planning instruction and provide the basis for student assessment. An excerpt from the California State Standards (http://www.cde.ca.gov) for grade four reading appears in Figure 1.3. It is interesting to note the degree of specificity contained in the standards. The open-endedness of "grade appropriate" designations provides room for flexibility.

DESIGNING POWERFUL LESSONS

The word "design" functions as a verb and a noun. As a verb, design is a process that means to draw, plan, or outline. As a noun, design is a product, a plan, an arrangement of details. Likewise, instructional design is both a process and a product. The teacher "draws" the instructional plan first by determining what learning standards will be taught and then deciding how the standards will be assessed. In other words: (1) what will students learn, and (2) what will be the evidence of their learning? Once these decisions are made, the teacher determines appropriate teaching strategies and methods, selects resource and learning materials, decides how students will be grouped, and finally, reviews and fine-tunes the entire plan. Instructional

GRADE FOUR LEARNING STANDARDS AS ENUNCIATED IN THE CALIFORNIA STATE STANDARDS DOCUMENT

Word Recognition (Grade Four)

1.1 Read narrative and expository text aloud with grade-appropriate fluency and accuracy and with appropriate pacing, intonation, and expression.

Vocabulary and Concept Development (Grade Four)

1.2 Apply knowledge of word origins, derivations, synonyms, antonyms, and idioms to determine the meaning of words and phrases.

1.3 Use knowledge of root words to determine the meaning of unknown words within a passage.

1.4 Know common roots and affixes derived from Greek and Latin and use this knowledge to analyze the meaning of complex words (e.g., international).

1.5 Use a thesaurus to determine related words and concepts.

1.6 Distinguish and interpret words with multiple meanings.

Reading Comprehension (Grade Four)

2.0 Students read and understand grade-level-appropriate material. They draw upon a variety of comprehension strategies as needed (e.g., generating and responding to Basic questions, making predictions, comparing information from several sources). The selections in Recommended Readings in Literature, Kindergarten Through Grade Eight illustrate the quality and complexity of the materials to be read by students. In addition to their regular school reading, students read one-half million words annually, including a good representation of grade-level-appropriate narrative and expository text (e.g., classic and contemporary literature, magazines, newspapers, online information).

Structural Features of Informational Materials (Grade Four)

2.1 Identify structural patterns found in informational text (e.g., compare and contrast, cause and effect, sequential or chronological order, proposition and support) to strengthen comprehension.

Comprehension and Analysis of Grade-Level-Appropriate Text (Grade Four)

2.2 Use appropriate strategies when reading for different purposes (e.g., full comprehension, location of information, personal enjoyment).

2.3 Make and confirm predictions about text by using prior knowledge and ideas presented in the text itself, including illustrations, titles, topic sentences, important words, and foreshadowing clues.

2.4 Evaluate new information and hypotheses by testing them against known information and ideas.

Figure 1.3

2.5 Compare and contrast information on the same topic after reading several passages or articles.

2.6 Distinguish between cause and effect and between fact and opinion in expository text.

2.7 Follow multiple-step instructions in a Basic technical manual (e.g., how to use computer commands or video games).

Literary Response and Analysis (Grade Four)

3.0 Students read and respond to a wide variety of significant works of children's literature. They distinguish between the structural features of the text and the literary terms or elements (e.g., theme, plot, setting, characters). The selections in Recommended Readings in Literature, Kindergarten Through Grade Eight illustrate the quality and complexity of the materials to be read by students.

Structural Features of Literature (Grade Four)

3.1 Describe the structural differences of various imaginative forms of literature, including fantasies, fables, myths, legends, and fairy tales.

Narrative Analysis of Grade-Level-Appropriate Text (Grade Four)

3.2 Identify the main events of the plot, their causes, and the influence of each event on future actions.

3.3 Use knowledge of the situation and setting and of a character's traits and motivations to determine the causes for that character's actions.

3.4 Compare and contrast tales from different cultures by tracing the exploits of one character type and develop theories to account for similar tales in diverse cultures (e.g., trickster tales).

3.5 Define figurative language (e.g., simile, metaphor, hyperbole, personification) and identify its use in literary works.

Figure 1.3, continued

design is not a linear process. During the planning phase, decisions are continually adjusted and modified as new ideas and insights present themselves. The final plan reflects the needs and interests of the students for whom it is developed and is a unique reflection of the teacher's style and expertise.

Basic Instructional Design

A BASIC PLANNING GUIDE

The Basic Instructional Design Planning Guide is a thinking process approach to guide decision-making for basic instructional planning. It is comprised of three sections: (1) Desired Results, (2) Lesson Design, and (3) Evidence of Learning. Each of the three sections includes three columns: Planning Questions and Decisions, Information and Data Sources, and Notes and Comments. The Planning Questions and Decisions column poses a series of key questions to guide and stimulate thinking during the planning process. The Information and Data Sources column lists the types of resources and data sources that will facilitate answering the questions in column one. The Notes and Comments column provides information that will further clarify and assist in answering questions in column one. A detailed explanation of each section follows.

Section 1
DESIRED RESULTS

Learning Standards

The process of instructional design begins with the learning standards—what students are expected to know and do. It is this desired end result that drives the planning process and provides the focus and direction for the lesson. Wiggins and McTighe (1998) tell us to begin with the end in mind—think first about the desired results.

Objective Objection

Some educators make too much of stating learning benchmarks (objectives) in such precise terms that they become confused with activities. There is a clear distinction and an obvious connection between a benchmark and an activity. The benchmark is what the student will know and be able to do as a result of engaging in the activity. We start with the standard or benchmark, determine what evidence will we acquire to determine whether the standard or benchmark is met, and then plan the activities that will get us to this end.

Basic Instructional Design

PLANNING GUIDE—BASIC INSTRUCTION

DESIRED RESULTS

Use these questions to plan a basic instructional design.

PLANNING QUESTIONS AND DECISIONS	INFORMATION AND DATA SOURCES	NOTES AND COMMENTS
1. What learning standards/ benchmarks will be taught?	District curriculum guides, district and state standards documents, student needs based on test data (formal and informal), school improvement goals, district goals, state initiatives	A decision regarding what is to be taught is made before completing the rest of the planning process.
2. What is the specific learning standard?		A clear statement of what students are to do provides clarity and focus in planning.
3. What assessment activities will enable students to demonstrate they have met the learning standard?	Recommended and required assessments, textbook materials	Planning for assessment is a recursive process. Assessment strategies and tools are tentatively outlined in the initial stages of instructional design, reconsidered and modified as the design emerges, and then finalized as the design is completed.
4. What performance expectations are there for students to show the extent of learning that has occurred?	District, state expectations for performance and/or teacher developed expectations	
5. How will students' difficulties be recognized along the way?	Formative assessments, observational techniques	
6. What assessment materials are available and what materials need to be developed?	Rubrics and assessments in district curriculum guides, teacher manuals, other sources	
7. How will assessment results be communicated to students and parents?	Report cards, grading scale, narrative report, conference, portfolio	Select the assessment strategy that is most appropriate. If the assessment results are to be incorporated into a grade, appropriate documentation should be made.

Section 1

DESIRED RESULTS
Planning Questions and Decisions
Science Class Grade 7

1. What learning standards will be taught?
The standard is part of the district curriculum in physical science, part of the sequence in understanding solutions. It aligns to state and NSTA standards.

2. What is the specific learning standard?
Students will distinguish between mixtures that are solutions and those that are not.

3. What assessment activities will enable students to demonstrate they have met the learning standard?
Students will enter findings and conclusions in their science log. A forced choice assessment will show what factual knowledge students have acquired. (I may have to modify the assessment in the text to include the additional information I wish to present.) Students will develop an outline for their presentation. (The presentation rubric will be used.)

4. What performance expectations are there for students to show the extent of learning that has occurred?
Science logs will have appropriate detail and diagrams. (Corrections are expected if necessary.)
Students will answer 80% of the questions on the forced choice test correctly. (Corrections are expected if necessary.)
Students will develop an outline for their presentation. (The presentation rubric will be used.)

5. How will students' difficulties be recognized along the way?
Student responses during class discussion will be noted to determine understanding. (I need to be sure to ask several questions during class discussion to ascertain students' understanding. I will use my classes list to note which students appear to need further assistance. They will be paired with a "stronger partner" for a study buddies activity.)

6. What assessment materials are available and what materials need to be developed?
Instructions for the experiments and a rubric describing levels of performance for the science log entries will be developed and discussed prior to the lesson.

7. How will assessment results be communicated to students and parents?
Students will receive a copy of the rubric showing the assessment of their science log with teacher comments.
Students will understand that the science log assessment and the forced choice test will be included in their quarterly report card grade.

Basic Instructional Design

Section 2

LESSON DESIGN

A lesson plan is what the teacher does to teach the learning standard. The components of a lesson plan are described below.

Opening

The opening of the lesson sets the stage for what is to follow. The "anticipation" that is created motivates students and peaks their interest (Hunter 1984). It activates students' schemata by tapping into their prior knowledge and making connections to new learning. Calling to mind what is already known is critical for learning. Jensen (2000) says that the more associations and connections one makes, the more firmly new information is "woven in neurologically." There is greater depth of meaning when new information is connected to existing knowledge. The lesson opening, therefore, should be structured to help students recall what they already know, understand the relevance of what they will learn, and be aware of what they will know and be able to do as a result of the learning activity. In other words, students should consciously connect new learning to previous learning (see Figure 1.4). The teacher facilitates this process through appropriate opening activities.

Teaching Strategies/Activities (Input)

Teaching strategies are selected based on the type of content to be taught and the needs and abilities of the students. They include demonstrating, modeling, explaining, questioning, and coaching. Teaching strategies are what the teacher does to develop background and set the stage for the learning activities students will engage in. The input provided at this point gives students enough information to proceed confidently with the learning tasks (see Figure 1.5). It does not preclude exploration and discovery on their part.

COMPONENTS OF AN EFFECTIVE LESSON PLAN

❏ Opening

❏ Teaching strategies/activities (input)

❏ Student activities

❏ Materials/resources

❏ Grouping pattern

❏ Monitoring student progress

❏ Ending/summary/reflection

Figure 1.4

Student Activities

In selecting or developing an instructional activity it is important to consider its "fit" with the learning standard and student needs and abilities. An instructional activity is always related to the learning standard—it is not an end in itself. To learn, a student engages in an activity. A learning activity may be as simple as reading a selection, or it may be a more complex activity such as gathering data from multiple sources for problem solving. Today, a plethora of instructional activities are offered in teaching manuals, professional journals, books, newsletters, software, and the Internet. Far more activities are available than can possibly be used by any given teacher or student. The teacher must be selective.

CONTENT-SPECIFIC EXAMPLES OF TEACHING INPUT

❏ Demonstrating pulley operation

❏ Modeling a think-aloud during a poetry reading

❏ Explaining the life cycle of a frog

❏ Questioning and discussing to elicit higher order thinking related to legislative decisions

❏ Coaching for sound articulation

Figure 1.5

Engaged Learning How students learn is just as important as what they learn. Student engagement is a high-priority consideration in instructional design. Danielson (1996, 95) states: "Engaging students in learning is the raison d'être of education. All other components are in the service of student engagement..." But engaged learning activities are not selected merely for their hands-on quality and potential for enjoyment. The purpose of engagement is to involve students in developing important concepts, skills, and processes. Engagement provides the condition in which concepts are made meaningful.

Types of Learning Activities Learning activities are designed to enable students to reach specified standards. This is not as simple as it may sound. Other considerations affect the design of learning activities. Student interest impacts motivation, which affects attention and retention (Cummings 1980). Therefore learning activities should be appealing and interesting to students. An appropriate level of challenge is necessary to maintain interest; therefore learning activities should be designed to meet a wide range of student needs.

It is apparent that some learning standards relate to simple information and fact acquisition. Other standards require the learner to relate, transform, or

 # Basic Instructional Design

PLANNING GUIDE—BASIC INSTRUCTION
DESIGN
Use these questions as a thinking guide to plan a basic instructional design.

Planning Questions and Decisions	Information and Data Sources	Notes and Comments
1. What are the learning standard/benchmarks to be achieved?	See section one of this planning guide.	
2. What is a motivating opening for the lesson?		
3. What strategies or activities will be used to teach the standard?		
4. What materials are needed to support and enhance learning?	Curriculum guides, teaching manuals, professional literature, best practices information, etc. are sources of information for lesson development.	
5. What is the appropriate use of technology?		
6. How will students be grouped for this activity?		
7. What opportunities will students have to reflect on their learning?		
8. How will student progress be monitored?		
9. What forms of additional practice may be necessary?		
10. How long will the lesson take?		
11. Are there any foreseeable pitfalls in this lesson?		
12. What alternatives are there if the lesson doesn't work out?		

Section 2

DESIGN
Planing Questions and Decisions
Science Class Grade 7

1. What are the learning standard/benchmarks to be achieved?
Students will distinguish between mixtures that are solutions and those that are not.

2. What is a motivating opening for the lesson?
Set up as a problem-solving activity related to a real-life application: forensic scientist working with a detective to solve a criminal case. Show two containers of liquid and how they would identify the one that has water and the one that contains another substance. Ask students why such identification is necessary or important. Record responses for later review.

3. What strategies or activities will be used to teach the standard?
Possibilities include: Review and develop background information through discussion, reading, research, questioning the teacher. Use KWL strategy. Invite a chemist from local industry to talk with students about real-life applications. Conduct demonstration or experiment. Use lab record/report activity.

4. What materials are needed to support and enhance learning?
Safety goggles, lab aprons, graduated cylinders, clear plastic glasses or beakers, stirring rods, six prepared mixtures (water/milk, water/sugar, water/oil, water/rubbing alcohol, water/drink mix, sand/salt)
For Tyndall effect: Flashlight, cardboard, metric ruler, pencil

5. What is the appropriate use of technology?
Students may keep notes on word processing program. The computer probe equipment is also a possibly . . . perhaps as a demostration.

6. How will students be grouped for this activity?
Students will work in groups of three for the lab experiment. The class as a whole will discuss findings and outcomes.

7. What opportunities will students have to reflect on their learning?
At the conclusion of the lesson, students will write on three new things they learned as a result of the lesson and how these three things have application to their everyday life. (This could be part of the assessment.)

8. How will student progress be monitored?
During lab work, the teacher will observe students and check for proper use of equipment and following directions. Spot checks of lab book entries will be made.

9. What forms of additional practice may be necessary?
Students who miss this session or need further input may review textbook diagrams and explanations of the Tyndall effect and solutions. A video disk segment on solutions may be viewed. Or, they could partner with another student to review science log entries.

10. How long will the lesson take?
Two class periods will be scheduled for this lesson. I may have to provide additional time to get all presentations in— or I could have just a few groups present. Other groups could present for other lessons.

11. Are there any foreseeable pitfalls in this lesson?
Students must perform the experiment carefully to obtain the desired results. Students will need teacher supervision and direction in carrying out the experiment to ensure safety and proper use of lab equipment. Extra mixtures will be available in case of spills.

12. What alternatives are there if the lesson doesn't work out?
A demonstration will be used if the student activity doesn't work out as planned. Students will observe and record their findings in their science logs.

Basic Instructional Design

DESIGNING LEARNING ACTIVITIES

Literal Learning. Literal learning defines a relatively simple activity for acquiring basic information and facts. The following are examples of literal learning activities:

- Name the steps in the scientific method.
- Identify the President of the United States during the Great Depression.
- Match the Generals to their Civil War battles.
- Identify given rocks and minerals.

Relational Learning. In relational learning students relate or connect information from one or more sources including their own background knowledge. Some examples of relational learning activities are

- Locate the ancient civilization of Mesopotamia on a modern-day map.
- Compare the population of Illinois and Chicago over time.
- Predict the next action in a story.

Transformational Learning. Transformational learning requires the student to transcribe or apply learning in a different way. Some examples of transformational learning activities are as follows:

- Rewrite the ending to a story.
- Demonstrate the operation of a simple machine.
- Dramatize a historical event.

Extensional Learning. Extensional learning activities ask students to take their learning and extend it using literal, relational, and transformational strategies to create, produce, originate, evaluate, and in other ways exhibit their learning in a unique way. Some examples are

- Critique a novel.
- Design a rubric for a learning task and use it to assess the task.
- Justify the actions of the main character in a story.

Figure 1.6

extend concepts. The wording of the learning standard is a guide in developing learning activities. The wording of the learning activity guides the students in the learning task

The categorization of learning into literal, relational, transformational, and extensional domains allows teachers to use the wording of state learning standards. The categories do overlap. Strictly defined, separate categories of learning activities are probably not possible, but understanding general categories of learning helps to focus planning of activities in relation to the learning standards (see Figure 1.6). An important caveat to this categorization of learning activities is that all students should participate in all types of learning. It would be a drastic mistake to treat these categories as a hierarchy in which students begin with literal learning, staying there until the teacher decides mastery is obtained, and then move on to the next category. Linear use of learning categories is neither indicated nor effective. It is contrary to theory and research, which suggests an overlap and integration of the various types of thinking (Good and Brophy 1997). It is not possible to totally isolate levels of thinking into separate compartments—they are interrelated and iterative (Ellis and Fouts 1997).

Describing Learning Activities A critical part of instructional planning is the description, explanation, or directions for a learning activity. The wording of the description is carefully chosen to convey precisely what students are to accomplish. Selecting appropriate terminology for the learning activity is necessary to design coherent and organized instruction. If the students are asked only to list events in chronological order, it is not fair to expect that they will analyze those events. If analysis behavior is expected, the terminology that conveys this expectation must be used. The key word in the description of an instructional activity is the linchpin and, therefore, must be carefully chosen. A list of suggested terms for learning activities is contained in Figure 1.7. Teachers may find it helpful to refer to this list in describing instructional activities.

DESIGNING LEARNING ACTIVITIES: TERMS TO USE

Use the following terms to help recognize the type of learning required in a standard and to design instructional activities that correspond to the learning standard.

Literal Learning

count	label	outline
define	list	quote
find	match	recall
identify	name	tell

Relational Learning

compare	differentiate	locate	restate
conclude	discuss	measure	review
contrast	explain	paraphrase	sequence
demonstrate	generalize	predict	show
describe	interpret	report	summarize

Transformational Learning

analyze	collect	diagram	rewrite
apply	compute	distinguish	select
change	debate	dramatize	separate
characterize	deduce	examine	use
choose	demonstrate	research	

Extensional Learning

appraise	criticize	judge	prioritize
assess	decide	justify	produce
choose	design	make up	propose
compose	develop	originate	prove
conclude	evaluate	perform	rank
construct	integrate	plan	rate
create	invent	pretend	

Figure 1.7

Basic Instructional Design

LEARNING ACTIVITIES

1. Graphic Organizers
Use graphic organizers to create mind maps for students, thereby strengthening learning and subsequent recall of material. When the graphic organizers are personalized to match the needs and backgrounds of the students, they become even more powerful. A slightly different twist is to use pictures or drawings instead of words to create a mind map.

2. Creative Retelling
Weave content information into a story using known genres such as fables, tall tales, songs, and myths. In this manner, the information is transformed into a different setting.

3. Peer Presenting
Use an "each one, teach one" model, or in some manner allow students to teach each other. Explaining strengthens understanding.

4. Model Making
Create models (two- or three-dimensional) to produce a concrete representation of an abstract concept.

5. Performance
Transform information or a concept into a performance using drama, music, or dance. Write about the solution to a math problem or create a poem about a science concept.

6. Role Playing
Provide opportunities for some students to assume the role of historical or fictional characters while other students take on the role of reporter in an interview activity that contributes to whole learning through a simulated experience.

Figure 1.8

Brain-Frame Activities Recent research into how the brain learns provides a rich source of information for teachers as they plan instruction. Teachers frame instruction around brain-compatible learning to maximize learning. Robin Fogarty (1997) tells us that brain-compatible classrooms differ from others in three major ways. First, brain-compatible learning is integrated, not isolated. Second, threat and anxiety are diminished, allowing students to function at high levels. And third, learning involves real or simulated "whole" experiences that tap into many ways of thinking, expressing, and doing. Teachers may use many effective brain-based strategies to deepen students' understanding. Figure 1.8 is adapted from the work of Eric Jensen (1996). Figure 1.9 shows the relationship of some brain-framed activities to the major thinking function they support.

Materials/Resources
The variety of instructional materials available is extensive and at times overwhelming. Learning resources and materials must, of course, be appropriate to the needs and interests of the students. Sometimes the only materials needed are a pencil and paper (or word processor). Other times, more extensive resources are needed for exploration and research. Generally the teacher selects learning resources for young learners. But as students take more responsibility for their learning, they begin to search out information and learning resources on their own. Guidance and support at

this stage helps students become independent learners and users of the vast number of resources at their disposal.

Although the practice is not as prevalent today as in the past, some schools use a commercial textbook program as the required curriculum. When this is the case, state or district learning standards are used as a filter in selecting what is important to teach from the textbook. A comparison of learning standards and textbook objectives points out instructional priorities and enables the teacher to eliminate some textbook material. This standards-driven approach makes the curriculum more manageable.

7. Debate, Discuss, Debrief
Provide opportunities for students to explain their thinking in a nonthreatening environment. Communication is the key for deepening understanding.

8. Game Making
Use a known game genre into which the new concepts and material are incorporated.

9. Presentations
Provide opportunities for students to use technology or visual aids, or to process information and transform it for others.

Activities such as those described above allow students to do something, to use concepts, ideas, strategies, and processes. This use and manipulation of material is the vehicle to deepen understanding by weaving it into existing knowledge.

Figure 1.8, continued

Technology-related materials can support and enhance student learning. However, as with all materials, those that are technology based should be carefully chosen. Technology to support teaching the learning standards is the foremost consideration. Some technology-based applications can include the following:

• explore a concept using video discs, computer software programs, or the Internet

• present a concept or idea using video discs, computer software, or presentational tools (PowerPoint, HyperStudio)

• analyze and sort data and information using database programs

• create artistic products using graphic and sound design

Other resources for learning extend beyond the classroom into the community. Partnerships with governmental agencies, local businesses, and professional organizations can be a source of extended learning opportunities for students. Joining resources helps build greater understanding of the relationship between schooling and real-world applications.

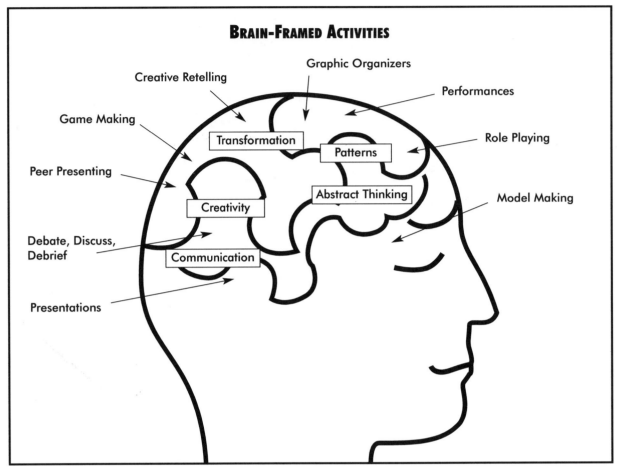

Figure 1.9

Grouping Pattern

The benefits of cooperative learning groups have been known for many years. Students in cooperative learning settings tend to perform better academically than students taught in individualistic or competitive settings (Johnson and Johnson 1984). Bellanca and Fogarty (1991) state: "Research on cooperative learning is overwhelmingly positive and the cooperative approaches are appropriate for all curriculum areas. The more complex the outcomes (high-order processing of information, problem solving, social skills and attitudes), the greater are the effects." There are times, however, when individual or whole group activities are appropriate. The key is to balance whole group teacher directed activities with cooperative learning groups (Zemelmann, Daniels, and Hyde 1993; Skowron 1990). Types of grouping arrangements in relation to instructional purposes are described in Figure 1.10.

GROUPING STUDENTS FOR INSTRUCTION		
GROUPING ARRANGEMENT	**DESCRIPTION**	**PURPOSE**
WHOLE CLASS	Students participate as a whole class with the teacher in a directed instructional activity	• presentation of information • demonstration/modeling of a process • outlining directions • sharing/reporting/communicating/presenting the work or cooperative groups
COOPERATIVE GROUPS	Students work with others in a cooperative group arrangement in which students are responsible for the group's activities. The teacher is a facilitator to the groups. Not all groups necessarily work on the same topic. A jigsaw approach specifies separate topics for each group with a whole class sharing at the conclusion of the project.	• solving a problem • exploring a topic • conducting an experiment • creating a model • developing a presentation • discussing concepts and ideas
INDEPENDENT WORK	The student focuses on a task to practice, reinforce, or extend specific learning or reflect on what they have learned. Independent work may be used when a student has missed some instruction or has not achieved the level or proficiency necessary. Independent work may also be appropriate when a student's capabilities show he/she would benefit from greater indepth exploration of a topic.	• practicing skills (math, spelling) • reading (literature selection or content information) • summarizing/reflecting on personal learning • independent research
PAIR AND SHARE	Students find it beneficial to work with one other student when they need tutoring or reinforcement of a learning concept or skill. Pair and Share also provides an opportunity for students to discuss a topic of study or class event in terms of feelings and attitudes.	• reading each others essays • listening to one another's stories • discussing what has been learned • discussing feelings and attitudes toward a given topic
SMALL GROUPS	Small group instruction is beneficial for teaching students who have common skill needs. The instruction is tailored to specifically meet the needs of the group. The groups are convened for a specific purpose and disbanded when the purpose is met.	• practicing letter/sound relationships • practicing correct use of the apostrophe in plural possessives • practicing fluency at the independent reading level • practicing the steps in using the calculator to perform specific operations • transposing music from key of C to key of F

Figure 1.10

Basic Instructional Design

Monitoring Student Progress

Monitoring students as they engage in a learning task is a crucial part of teaching. It is important for students to receive feedback on their progress throughout the learning activity. At times encouragement or positive affirmation is all that is needed. At other times clarification or instructional guidance is necessary to prevent misunderstandings. When confused, some students willingly ask for help. Other students do not. And still others do not even know they are confused. Monitoring all students is important to obtain diagnostic feedback and determine when intervention through reteaching or additional practice is necessary.

There are several ways to monitor students, ranging from observation in the classroom setting to performance tests and quizzes. Some general questions the teacher may use during monitoring are as follows:

Does the student exhibit confusion?

Is the student off task?

Has the student finished too soon or not soon enough?

Does the student understand the directions?

Is there some prior knowledge or prerequisite information the student needs?

Does the student's response indicate understanding?

A checklist may be used to monitor student progress during a learning activity. The checklist contains key criteria against which the students are observed (Burke 1994). A sample checklist for informational reading at the elementary level appears in Figure 1.11. The checklist will help determine which students have common difficulties. These students may then be grouped for reteaching, reinforcement, or practice activities.

Another form of student monitoring is through direct questioning on what is being learned. Questioning may be through a verbal exchange between teacher and student or in written form, through quizzes, summaries, or reflections. The type of monitoring a teacher chooses to do depends on the demands of the learning situation and the level of complexity and difficulty of the learning standards. Generally, more complex learning is better monitored through observation and questioning. Literal learning is more easily monitored through written quizzes and tests.

OBSERVATION CHECKLIST: READING FOR INFORMATION

Name																					
Uses prediction																					
Visualization apparent through descriptive illustration																					
Understands descriptive text																					
Recalls sequence and order																					
Compares and contrasts ideas presented in text																					
Explains cause/effect relationships																					
States opinion and gives reasons																					
Connects sources of information																					
Links reading to prior knowledge																					
Uses inferential thinking																					
Self-corrects																					
Exhibits independence																					

3 = Needs further instruction
2 = Shows developing understanding
1 = Demonstrates understanding

Figure 1.11

Ending/Summary/Reflection

When one links new learning to prior knowledge, one's mental map of information, concepts, skills, processes, attitudes, values, and beliefs related to a topic is expanded. This mental map is the schema or linked collection of related thoughts and ideas and is the operating base within which new information is integrated. Schema is expanded and understanding deepened through metacognitive processing and reflection. Seifert (1999) states that reflection is the partner of experience. Reflection and experience lead us to construct meaning. It is therefore important that students have opportunities for metacognitive processing throughout and especially at the conclusion of a learning experience. Notebook journals, audio journals, and sketchpads are some means for students to reflect and record the impact of their learning and thinking.

Practice Activities/Assignments

Not all students progress at the same pace. Monitoring and observation will indicate which students need more instruction or practice. For these students, it is appropriate to provide additional activities to reinforce learning. Practice activities should be interesting, well designed, and assigned only as necessary.

Section 3

EVIDENCE OF LEARNING

The purpose of assessment is to determine what the student has learned in relation to the learning standard. Since assessment is aligned to a learning standard, classroom instruction likewise must be aligned to that standard. Alignment of learning standards, instructional activities, and the assessment ensures that students are assessed on what was taught. If the standard is to identify rocks and minerals by their appearance, then students are assessed as they look at rocks and minerals and tell what they are. The teaching/learning activities that occur prior to the assessment provide input and practice on the physical appearance of rocks and minerals and how to identify them. When this is the case, there is no need for additional "test prep." The learning activities themselves are the preparation—and in some cases, may even be the assessment.

Assessment Strategies

The learning standard is the basis for assessment. Assessment strategies are formulated in the initial stage of planning and reconsidered and finalized with the completed instructional plan. The type of assessment selected will vary according to the type of learning that is expected.

In the broadest sense, assessments may be classified as selected response or performance based. Selected response assessments include the pencil-paper "traditional" forms of testing, i.e., true-false, multiple choice, short answer.

These assessments are useful in determining the student's content knowledge related to facts, information, and processes. Performance-based assessments are those that allow students to demonstrate what they can do with the learning they have acquired. Performance-based assessments include writing an essay, conducting research, preparing a report, presenting a demonstration, singing, playing a musical instrument, and performing a physical activity.

Students want to know how they will be assessed and evaluated. Parents also want to know what their student is learning and how he or she is progressing. Assessment tools such as rubrics and checklists help students understand what is to be learned by pointing out criteria and performance levels. They also clearly convey information about expectations and progress to parents (Burke 1994). When students and parents know the criteria and expectations, student performance often improves.

Basic Instructional Design

Section 3

PLANNING GUIDE—BASIC INSTRUCTION
EVIDENCE OF LEARNING
Use these questions as a thinking guide to plan a basic instructional design.

Planning Questions and Decisions	Information and Data Sources	Notes and Comments
1. How will students demonstrate their learning?	See curriculum resource information and best practices information related to types of assessment: criterion referenced assessment, performance assessment, observation, standardized	
2. How will the assessment be scored?	Consider use of a rubric, template, or Scantron scoring.	
3. How will learning be reported?	Consider appropriate types of feedback to students, use of a grading scale, parent reports, report cards, portfolios, etc. If feasible, electronic data may also be useful.	Refer to your planning notes in section one as you finalize decisions regarding assessment.
4. How will the assessment results be used?		Use assessment results to determine student strengths and weaknesses and plan the next lessons.

Section 3

EVIDENCE OF LEARNING
Planning Questions and Decisions

1. How will the students demonstrate their learning?
Science log entry of experiment—steps and conclusions
Forced choice test (20 items)
Present report to class

2. How will the assessment be scored?
Rubric
Answer key: (20 items, 5 points each). Sign up to use scantron for scoring.

3. How will the assessment be reported?
Copy of rubric showing performance level will be returned to students. Teacher comments will be included as appropriate.
Go over test items with students. Grades will be determined according to the school-wide grading scale.
Copy of rubric showing performance level will be returned to students. Teacher comments will be included as appropriate.

4. How will the assessment results be used?
Determine which students need additional practice. Include results in quarterly report card grade. Students make revisions as necessary.
Determine which students need reinforcement of factual information. Students make corrections as necessary. Include results in quarterly report card grade.
The rubric will provide feedback to the student. A total of 5 points will be included in the quarterly report card grade.

Basic Instructional Design

USING THE BASIC INSTRUCTIONAL DESIGN PLANNING GUIDE

The Basic Instructional Design Planning Guide is a thinking process approach to instructional planning. Preservice and novice teachers will find it helpful to follow all the steps in the guide. Understanding the thinking process underlying instructional design makes subsequent planning easier and provides a foundation for planning more complex instruction. Below are suggestions for using the planning guide.

1. Read the planning guide in its entirety

It is good practice to become thoroughly familiar with the planning guide before using it. Doing so saves time in the long run. Get the "big picture" in mind before filling in the details.

2. Think it through

Begin with Section 1: Desired Results. Think about the questions in column one and write down your thoughts and reactions. Consult the data and information sources suggested in column two and note the reminders and supplemental information in column three. Add notes and comments for later reference. Continue through Section 2: Lesson Design and Section 3: Evidence of Learning.

3. Synthesize the information

The thinking process in step two above provides a great deal of information which now must be synthesized into a coherent plan for instruction. The Basic Lesson Plan Form (Figure 1.12) is a synthesis and summary of the decisions made in working through the Basic Instructional Design Planning Guide. It is an action plan and a presentational overview for classroom instruction. An example of how this guide has been used by a seventh-grade science teacher appears in Figure 1.13.

BASIC LESSON PLAN FORM

LEARNING STANDARD/BENCHMARKS (concepts, skills, processes)

LESSON DESIGN Opening (outcomes/purpose/expectations)	MATERIALS/RESOURCES	STUDENT GROUPING ARRANGEMENT
Teaching Strategies/Activities (demonstration, modeling, explanation, directions, etc.)		
Student Activities		
Closing (connections/summary/reflection)		
PRACTICE ACTIVITIES/ASSIGNMENTS		
MONITORING STUDENT PROGRESS (ongoing)		
ASSESSMENT OF STUDENT LEARNING		**EXPECTATIONS**

Figure 1.12

Basic Instructional Design

LESSON PLAN — GRADE 7 SCIENCE

LEARNING STANDARD (concepts, skills, processes)
Students will differentiate mixtures that are solutions and those that are not.

LESSON DESIGN	MATERIALS/RESOURCES	STUDENT GROUPING ARRANGEMENT
Opening (outcomes/purpose/expectations) Describe problem scenario: A forensic scientist is working with a detective to solve a criminal case. Show two beakers. Ask: How can the scientist tell which beaker contains water and which contains a mixture of salt and water? Discuss responses. Record responses for later review. Ask: Why is it important to be able to identify substances?	Beakers/mixtures Chart paper, markers	Whole class
Teaching Strategies/Activities (demonstration, modeling, explanation, directions, etc.) Describe lab set up and activity. (Refer to Lab Activity manual.) Review lab safety. Distribute/review experiment procedure.		
Student Activities Complete lab activity. Record findings in lab manual.	Safety glasses, lab aprons, graduated cylinders, clear beakers, stirring rods, six prepared mixtures, testing substances as listed in activity manual.	Three students per group (pre-arranged by teacher) Lab manual entries — individual
Closing (connections/summary/reflection) Groups 1, 2, 3 to report findings. Compare results. Verbalize conclusions. Review opening activity discussion. Discuss what was learned in the lab activity. Record two or more important concepts from this experiment in lab manual.		Whole class Lab manual entry — individual
PRACTICE ACTIVITIES/ASSIGNMENTS View video disc segment on this experiment and record results in lab manual.		Individual or small group – depending on who is absent. Arrange with resource center for viewing and completion of work.
MONITORING STUDENT PROGRESS (ongoing) Informal observation and coaching during group work.		
ASSESSMENT OF STUDENT LEARNING 1. In small groups, students will use the rubric to evaluate their lab manual entries. 2. Twenty item completion test on content.		**EXPECTATIONS** Students will meet or exceed all categories on rubric. Students will achieve 80% correct to meet expectations, 90% to exceed expectations.

Figure 1.13

When a novice teacher uses the planning guide over and over, he or she becomes familiar and comfortable with the planning process. With experience the teacher is able to take shortcuts in planning by using the lesson plan form without filling out the planning guide. This shortcut is possible when the planning questions are practiced and well known.

REFLECTIVE PRACTICE

Merely following an outline or filling in a template is not sufficient to develop expertise in planning powerful lessons. Planning is a metacognitive, reflective process where the teacher thinks, reflects, adjusts, redirects, fiddles, and fine-tunes the various components until a powerful lesson plan emerges. When reflection is an intrinsic part of the instructional planning process and teachers take time to analyze their planning efforts, they learn through their experiences, and future planning becomes more effective and efficient.

What Costa (1991) called "inner dialogue" is essential to professional growth, change, and improvement. Use the Inner Dialogue page that follows to reflect on planning actions, attempts, and results of using the Basic Instructional Design. Be open-minded but skeptical. Consider pros and cons, benefits, and challenges. Look beyond what was accomplished to why and how it was accomplished.

Basic Instructional Design

INNER DIALOGUE

Take time to reflect on the process you have gone through to plan basic instruction. Keep in mind that you are developing planning skills that will become stronger with experience and practice. As with all learning, reflecting on your experience will deepen your understanding. At some point, you will feel comfortable taking some short cuts and you will understand why and how you are able to do so. Keep your notes and refer to them when you plan again.

Fact This is what I did in the planning process.	**React** This is what I think about it and how I might change or modify it.
Some new learning	
Some benefits	
Some challenges	

Monday 10/2	Tuesday 10/3	Wednesday 10/4		Thursday 10/5	Friday 10/6	Notes
		Group Presentations →		8:15—9:05 Use attentive listening w/read aloud (SSR)	State testing →	Schedule Conferences
8:15—9:05 Assign E-pen pals Silent Reading	Group Presentations Assign H.W.	Graph results of survey (pictograph) →		9:10—10:00 Specials— P.E.	↓	
9:10—10:00 Organize Coop. groups	Specials— Math Committee Meeting	Role Play Group 1—Sc. 1 Group 2—Sc. 2		10:05—10:55 E-pen pal reports (SSR)	H →	
10:05—10:55 Guest panel for PBL examination Assign H.W.	Guest panel for PBL examination Assign H.W.	N ↗		11:00—11:50 C Supervision	→	
11:00—11:50 L Supervision	U	Specials →		11:55—12:45 • Collage • move to assigned centers (SSR)	Specials →	
11:55—12:45 Specials	Class disc.— conflict and feelings in lit. Assign H.W.	→		12:50—1:40 Turn in community survey materials (SSR)	State testing	
12:50—1:40 Staff Meeting Assign proj. for next mo.	Lab time Use Internet sources →	Bridging snapshots to explain scientific process →		1:40—2:35 Re-group/move seats (SSR)	↓	
1:40—2:35 Group Presentations	Begin to formulate/create motiles Assign H.W.	Cont. wk on motiles—Each group Give prog. report				

Basic Instructional Design

BASIC LESSON PLAN FORM

LEARNING STANDARD/BENCHMARKS (concepts, skills, processes)	MATERIALS/RESOURCES	STUDENT GROUPING ARRANGEMENT
LESSON DESIGN Opening (outcomes, purpose, expectations)		
Teaching Strategies/Activities (demonstration, modeling, explanation, directions, etc.)		
Student Activities		
Closing (connections/summary/reflection)		
PRACTICE ACTIVITIES/ASSIGNMENTS		
MONITORING STUDENT PROGRESS (ongoing)		
ASSESSMENT OF STUDENT LEARNING		EXPECTATIONS

SkyLight Professional Development

OBSERVATION CHECKLIST—READING FOR OBSERVATION

3 = Needs further instruction
2 = Shows developing understanding
1 = Demonstrates understanding

Name	Uses prediction	Visualization apparent through descriptive illustration	Understands descriptive text	Recalls sequence and order	Compares and contrasts ideas presented in text	Explains cause/effect relationships	States opinion and gives reasons	Connects sources of information	Links reading to prior knowledge	Uses inferential thinking	Self-corrects	Exhibits independence

Basic Instructional Design

Section 1

DESIRED RESULTS
Planning Questions and Decisions for Basic Instruction

1. What learning standards/benchmarks will be achieved?

2. What is the specific learning standard?

3. What assessment activities will enable students to demonstrate they have met the learning standard?

4. What performance expectations are there for students to show the extent of learning that has occurred?

5. How will students' difficulties be recognized along the way?

6. What assessment materials are available and what materials need to be developed?

7. How will assessment results be communicated to students and parents?

SkyLight Professional Development

Section 2

DESIGN
Planning Questions and Decisions for Basic Instruction

1. What learning standard/benchmarks will be achieved?

2. What is a motivating opening for the lesson?

3. What strategies or activities will be used to teach the standard?

4. What materials are needed to support and enhance learning?

5. What is the appropriate use of technology?

6. How will students be grouped for this activity?

7. What opportunities will students have to reflect on their learning?

8. How will student progress be monitored?

9. What forms of additional practice may be necessary?

10. How long will the lesson take?

11. Are there any foreseeable pitfalls in this lesson?

12. What alternatives are there if the lesson doesn't work out?

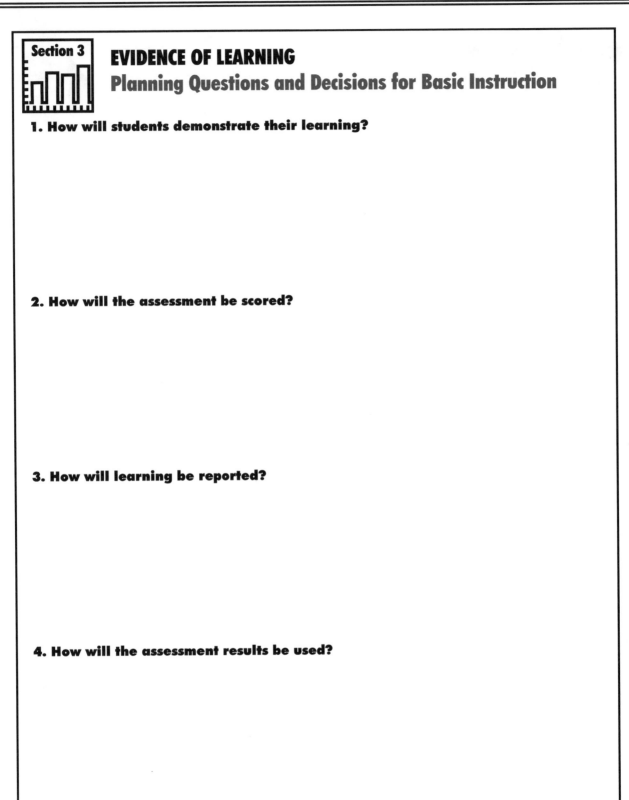

Section 3 **EVIDENCE OF LEARNING**
Planning Questions and Decisions for Basic Instruction

1. How will students demonstrate their learning?

2. How will the assessment be scored?

3. How will learning be reported?

4. How will the assessment results be used?

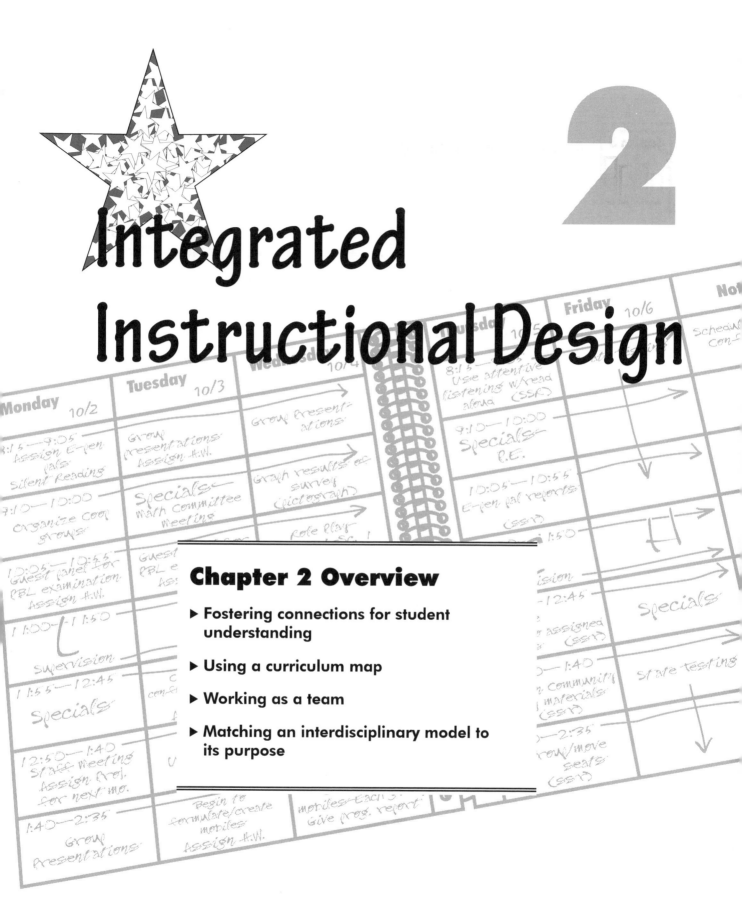

Integrated Instructional Design

2

Chapter 2 Overview

▶ Fostering connections for student understanding

▶ Using a curriculum map

▶ Working as a team

▶ Matching an interdisciplinary model to its purpose

Integrated Instructional Design

Integrated instruction, sometimes referred to as thematic instruction, problem-based instruction, or experiential learning, most likely has its roots in the progressive education movement of the early 1900s (Rippa 1988, Drake 1993). John Dewey emphasized the advantages of engaging students in real-world experiences and criticized instructional methods that focused learning into separate, isolated compartments. His belief in the importance of experience as a method of teaching is shown in the following statement.

All things are connected...
—Chief Seattle

Our whole policy of compulsory education rises or falls with our ability to make school life an interesting and absorbing experience to the child. In one sense, there is no such thing as compulsory education. We can have compulsory physical attendance at school; but education comes only through willing attention to and participation in school activities. It follows that the teacher must select these activities with reference to the child's interests, powers, and capacities. In no other way can she guarantee that the child will be present (Dewey 1913, ix).

AN INTEGRATED APPROACH TO LEARNING

Integrated instruction combines learning standards from different content areas within the same lesson or unit of study. The learning standards are connected through activities and tasks in a logical manner so students are able to understand relationships among the standards and the purpose of their learning. Assessment of student progress is likewise connected and embedded in the activities. An integrated approach to learning provides continuity and order for students. It helps them make sense of and see associations among the seeming randomness of educational objectives (Zemmelman, Daniels, and Hyde 1993). Genuine learning occurs as students see the connections among concepts and weave these connections into their own scheme of meaning (Beane 1993). An integrated curriculum helps students construct knowledge for themselves (Burke 1994). Integrated learning designs range from the combination of a few learning standards to total curriculum integration based on a major theme.

WHY INTEGRATED INSTRUCTION IS A GOOD IDEA

Understanding relationships and connections is far more valuable than knowing isolated bits and pieces of information (Withrow, Long, and Marx 1999). Caine and Caine (1991) explain that the brain searches for patterns and connections within experiences to make sense of the world. Experiences that provide opportunities for students to make connections are likely to provide more lasting and deeper learning. The propensity of the human brain to search for patterns of meaning is the reasoning behind integrated instruction (Jensen 2000). Shanahan (1997) reports that student motivation in integrated learning settings is greater than in traditional settings, and integrated instruction produces positive attitudes toward learning. While few empirical studies have been done to test the effectiveness of integrated learning, proponents of this approach base their support on the positive experiences and observations of classrooms where integrated learning flourishes (Guthrie and McCann 1997). The theoretical basis for integrated instruction is also found in constructivist theory, which explains that learning occurs as a person builds meaning through direct experience (Ellis and Fouts 1997).

> The propensity of the human brain to search for patterns of meaning is the reasoning behind integrated instruction.

BENEFITING FROM BEST PRACTICE MODELS

The predominant factors that seem to deter teachers from using an integrated instructional approach are lack of time for planning and instruction, professional development,

---

INTEGRATED INSTRUCTION

Ellis and Fouts (1997) make several educationally sound arguments for integrated instruction:

Psychological/developmental—Learning occurs best when individuals see the connections among concepts.

Sociocultural—Current curriculum, especially at the secondary level, does not address the needs, interests, and capabilities of today's students. Updating through curriculum integration has the potential to resolve these inadequacies.

Motivational—Interest and motivation are enhanced through integrated learning activities when students see the purpose of their learning and are able to choose their learning activities.

Pedogogical—The traditional curriculum has become overloaded. Teachers are hard pressed to cover all the so-called essentials and do so in a meaningful way. Integrating learning concepts makes better use of classroom time.

Integrated Instructional Design

and practical models. Even when teachers are convinced of the effectiveness of integrated instruction and motivated to use it, the lack of practical models may discourage them (Gehrke 1993).

Teachers need time to plan, especially with one another, to integrate standards across content areas. Otherwise the task may be too monumental for any one teacher to assume (Jacobs 1991a). Just as students benefit from working in teams, so do teachers when there is a feeling of shared responsibility.

In spite of the advantages associated with integrated instruction, American education today, for the most part, remains structured around separate disciplines or content areas (Bean 1993, Ellis and Fouts 1997, Jacobs 1991a). At the high school level, the student's day is an assortment of seven or eight unrelated, disjointed time periods (Zemmelman, Daniels, and Hyde 1993). And, in the classroom where the curriculum is translated into instruction, instruction is most likely to be a series of isolated lessons. Some high schools have shown progress toward integrated learning by combining English, literature, history, and civics in an American Studies course. Most often, this type of course is team taught by content area certified teachers.

Students need time to actively engage in learning, process their learning, and reflect on their learning (Caine and Caine 1991; Fogarty 1996). The traditional forty-five minute time period schedule, predominant in today's high schools, does not lend itself to the type of teaching that promotes integrated, connected learning. Many teachers report that with a forty-five minute time period, there is little they can do other than the traditional lecture, question, respond strategy. Some middle schools and high schools have changed from the shorter periods to longer blocks of time to promote more connected learning through integrated instruction (Canady and Rettig 1996). Longer blocks of time enable teachers to actively involve students in learning.

If teachers are to change the way they teach, they need ongoing professional development (Withrow, Long, and Marx 1999). Effective professional development not only points out best practices, but also provides practical,

> Students need time to actively engage in learning, process their learning, and reflect on their learning.

realistic models—a structure for learning, transferring, and applying new approaches (Moye 1997). Professional development related to integrated instruction prepares teachers with strategies for successful implementation.

HOW TO BEGIN

Integrating the curriculum can be a formidable task, but it becomes more manageable if approached in an organized, step-by-step manner. A clearly defined rationale for using integrated instruction and an organized plan to facilitate smooth implementation must exist. As Relan and Kimpston (1993) point out, there should be clear reasons for selecting an integrated approach over some other approach. Brophy and Alleman (1991) likewise explain that teachers must be selective and astute in planning curriculum integration and beware of integration merely for the sake of integration. There should be a logical connection among the learning standards incorporated into the integrated plan and a clear, direct connection between the standards and the teaching and learning activities.

One of the first planning steps in designing integrated instruction is to construct a calendar curriculum map that lists the topics of study in various content areas and their sequence through the school year. Heidi Hayes Jacobs (1991b, 1997) describes a process of calendar curriculum mapping where teachers plot out the topics that are being taught. Each teacher writes down the major topics of study for his or her content area for each month of the school year. An example of such a calendar curriculum map is shown in Figure 2.1. It is a general overview showing what is taught and when it is taught. This map is an "inventory" of content covered at a particular grade level. This approach to designing integrated instruction begins with the current curriculum rather then starting from scratch.

Each of the topics on the curriculum calendar map is associated with specific learning standards. These must be identified and analyzed to determine overlaps and gaps so that adjustments can be made accordingly. Realigning

> Professional development related to integrated instruction prepares teachers with strategies for successful implementation.

Integrated Instructional Design

	Language Arts	**Social Studies**	**Science**	**Mathematics**
September	*Diary of Anne Frank*	The Westward Movement	Interactions and Changes	Problem Solving
October				Decimals
November	*Sarah Plain and Tall*	The Civil War	Diversity of Living Things	Data Analysis
December				Fractions
January	*To Kill a Mockingbird*	Industrial Revolution World War I	Force and Motion	Integers
February	*Johnny Tremain*		The Restless Earth	Ratio/Percents
March	*Paul Bunyan and the Winter of the Blue Snow*	The Great Depression	The Universe	Probability
April		World War II		Geometry
May	*The Raven and the Coming of Daylight*		Solutions	Intro to Algebra

CURRICULUM CALENDAR MAP FOR GRADE 7 TEAM PRELIMINARY LISTING PRIOR TO ALIGNMENT

Figure 2.1

the standards in this way and connecting them to mutually supportive learning activities is central to planning for integrated instruction. The alignment of standards makes it easier to plan integrated lessons and units of study.

Some learning standards have a natural connection, some are mutually reinforcing, and some can be threaded through a "big idea" or theme. Examples of types of standard connections are described below.

Some learning standards have a natural connection. For example, combining graphing with reporting scientific data not only makes sense in terms of saving instructional time, it is also more meaningful for students. They use graphing for a real purpose.

Some learning standards are mutually reinforcing. For example, when students write about something they have read (short story) or done (science experiment), they communicate their comprehension and understanding and reinforce their writing skills.

Some learning standards are threaded through a "big idea." For example, the study of people in societies combines learning standards from history, geography, government and civics, economics, anthropology, and sociology (Lewis 1993). The focus or emphasis during such a unit of study may shift from history to economics to sociology depending on the learning standards being addressed.

The curriculum mapping procedure may also bring to light needed or desired changes in content. The planning process requires teachers to be open-minded and flexible in making changes to the curriculum. For example, the fact that a particular novel has always been taught at a particular time and grade level is not justification for having it remain so when another novel or reading activity may better reinforce and contribute to integrated learning.

Curriculum integration may be approached in a variety of ways. Robin Fogarty (1991) presents ten models of curriculum integration approaches. She begins by explaining the traditional, separate disciplines model and then describes the integrated models as summarized in Figure 2.2.

FOGARTY'S MODEL OF CURRICULUM INTEGRATION

Fragmented—The traditional model of separate and distinct disciplines, which fragments the subject areas.

Connected—Within each subject area, course content is connected topic to topic, concept to concept, one year's work to the next, and relates ideas(s) explicitly.

Nested—Within each subject area, the teacher targets multiple skills: a social skill, a thinking skill, and a content specific skill.

Sequenced—Topics or units of study are rearranged and sequenced to coincide with one another. Similar ideas are taught in concert while remaining separate subjects.

Shared—Shared planning and teaching take place in two disciplines in which overlapping concepts or ideas emerge as organizing elements.

Webbed—A major theme is selected and the learning concepts of all the disciplines are examined to determine a "fit" with the major theme. Once the learning concepts are outlined, instructional activities are designed around them. (This is probably the most popular approach to integrating the curriculum.)

Threaded—The metacurricular approach threads thinking skills, social skills, multiple intelligences, technology, and study skills through the various disciplines.

Integrated—This interdisciplinary approach matches subjects with overlaps in topics and concepts, using some team teaching in an authentic integrated model.

Immersed—The disciplines become part of the learner's lens of expertise; the learner filters all content through this lens and becomes immersed in his or her own experience.

Networked—The learner filters all learning through the expert's eye and makes internal connections that lead to external networks of experts in related fields.

Figure 2.2

Integrated Instructional Design

Any of the models described above may be used to integrate the curriculum. A discussion among staff members on the pros and cons of these models helps to build common understandings and to develop a rationale for using a particular type of integrated instruction.

SkyLight Professional Development

Integrated Instructional Design
A PLANNING GUIDE FOR INTEGRATED INSTRUCTION

The Planning Guide for Integrated Instructional Design is a thinking process approach to guide decision-making for integrated instructional planning. It guides the teacher through the preliminary planning process using a series of key questions that are referenced to resources and pertinent information and comments. It is comprised of three sections: (1) Desired Results, (2) Lesson Design, and (3) Evidence of Learning. Each section has three columns: Planning Questions and Decisions, Planning Resources, and Notes and Comments.

The Planning Questions and Decisions column poses a series of key questions. The Planning Resources column lists the types of resources and data sources that will facilitate answering the questions in column one. The Notes and Comments column provides information that will further clarify and assist in answering questions in column one. A detailed explanation of each section follows.

Section 1 — DESIRED RESULTS

Planning Question and Decision 1:
MAKE THE COMMITMENT

The first question to be addressed is why integrated instruction will best serve the students. A written statement affirming the value and use of integrated learning serves as a rationale, gives direction to the teaching staff, and communicates to parents and the community what students learn and how they will learn it.

Planning Question and Decision 2:
CONSTRUCT THE CURRICULUM CALENDAR MAP

Once an affirmative decision to use integrated instruction is made, all teachers involved participate in developing the curriculum calendar map. While it is possible for one teacher to design and implement integrated instruction for his or her classroom, the planning effort is more efficient when many teachers are involved. A schoolwide effort to integrate instruction includes all staff members in planning. A grade-level effort includes all teachers of that grade level.

Planning Questions and Decisions 3 and 4:
TRANSLATE CONTENT TO LEARNING STANDARDS

The next step in the planning process involves taking an in-depth look at the content and topics entered on the curriculum calendar map and translating them into learning standards. The Integrated Instructional Planner, Part 1 (Figure 2.3) is used to document the learning standards within the content areas that cluster around a major learning theme. This highlights and enables correction of redundancies and gaps in the curriculum. The priority of the learning standards is considered and decisions made regarding which standards are to be emphasized. Standards designated as having a high priority due to a weakness determined through student assessment data receive greater emphasis and focus during instruction.

For integrated instruction to be effective, students must understand the patterns of meaning that are intended (Jensen 2000). Therefore, students must have a clear understanding of what they are expected to learn (learning standards) within the integrated activity. The Integrated Instructional Planner Part 1 may be shared with students to enable them to understand the purpose of the integrated activities. For young students, the standards may be rewritten and presented in using simple terminology.

Planning Question and Decision 5:
CONSIDER ASSESSMENT STRATEGIES

Student assessment in an integrated setting is best accomplished as a performance task related to the actual learning activities. Any instructional activity may serve as an assessment when the teacher designs a rubric for it. Embedding assessment in instruction is both effective and efficient. Assessment is directly related to what is being learned, and it is not a separate activity that requires additional time or preparation.

Planning Question and Decision 6:
MONITOR STUDENT PROGRESS

An important part of teaching is observing and monitoring students' progress as they engage in learning activities. Planning to do so ensures that this important part of the teaching and learning process is conducted.

Planning Question and Decision 7:
COMMUNICATING ACHIEVEMENT

Achievement measures how well the learning standards have been met. The manner in which learning progress and achievement are communicated may vary from written reports to informal conversations. Students need feedback on their progress with information on how to improve. Parents want to know how their students are progressing and how to help them.

Integrated Instructional Design

Section 1	PLANNING GUIDE—INTEGRATED INSTRUCTION
	DESIRED RESULTS

Use these questions to plan an integrated instructional design.

PLANNING QUESTIONS AND DECISIONS	INFORMATION AND DATA SOURCES	NOTES AND COMMENTS
1. How and why will teaching and learning be more effective if learning standards are integrated within lessons rather than taught separately?	Review professional literature on integrated instruction as it relates to the district curriculum, state standards, student needs based on test data (formal and informal), school improvement goals, district and school goals.	It is important to have a rationale for integrated instruction that is clearly communicated to parents and other stakeholders.
2. What connections exist among the learning standards?	Refer to the Curriculum Calendar Map example (Figure 2.1)	Determine what relationships already exist among the curriculum areas by constructing a curriculum map. Don't try to force objectives to fit into an integrated design. There should be a natural, easy coordination.
3. How will learning standards be organized and documented?	Refer to the Integrated Instruction Planner samples in Figures 2.3 and 2.4.	Construct a graphic showing the relationships of the learning standards across the content areas.
4. What standards are a higher priority than others?	Review student strengths and weaknesses as shown in assessment data.	Determine the level of importance of the standards. Higher priority standards should be given greater instructional time.
5. How will the learning standards be assessed? (Are combined or embedded assessments feasible?) **6. What assessment materials are available and what materials need to be developed?**	Review any required and optional assessments. Review rubrics and assessments in district curriculum guides, teacher manuals, other sources.	Planning for assessment is a recursive process. Assessment strategies and tools are tentatively outlined in the initial stages of instructional design, reconsidered and modified as the design emerges, and then finalized with the finished product.
7. How will students' difficulties be recognized along the way?	Consider the use of formative assessments and observational techniques.	
8. How will assessment results be communicated to students and parents?	Consider report cards, grading scale, portfolios, and other means.	

Section 1

DESIRED RESULTS—INTEGRATED
Planning Questions and Decisions

Grade 5 Team

1. How and why will teaching and learning be more effective if learning standards are integrated within lessons rather than taught separately?

We have a modified departmentalized arrangement for grade five students. It seems we have been teaching the same concepts in several different classes. If we plan together we can eliminate this redundancy and have time for teaching other concepts. Also, our students will experience connections among the content areas and be involved in using information across the curriculum. We hope this will strengthen their learning and make it more meaningful.

2. What connections exist among the learning standards?

The standards we have identified are from reading, writing, listening/speaking, science, social studies, and fine arts. At this time we did not see a connection to any math standards or physical education standards but would like to build other units to incorporate these areas also. We, as teachers, are beginning to build connections in our minds. Perhaps this is the first step to helping our students do the same.

3. How will learning standards be organized and documented?

We are going to use the Integrated Instructional Planner, Part I as a starting point. We discussed how we would use this tool to provide our students with an overview of what they will learn. We might set up an assembly arrangement to kick this off.

4. What standards are a higher priority than others?

The way we planned this out, all the standards are important. Students will need some out of class time to work on their computer reports so we will need to plan for that. Otherwise, too much class time will be used.

5. How will the learning standards be assessed? (Are combined or embedded assessments feasible?)

We like the idea of using rubrics for the activities along the way rather than having a separate final assessment. The students' reports and presentations will be their final assessment. We reviewed the state standards and the district level requirements. We have even gone beyond with our fine arts standards. Marilyn (art teacher) convinced us that it would be a good connection to all the other content area standards.

6. What assessment materials are available and what materials need to be developed?

We have a writing rubric developed by the teachers that we will use for the writing components. We will develop a rubric with the students for the multi-media presentations they will do. They will use the rubric to evaluate their own presenation. We're cautious about having them evaluate each other. We'll see how it goes.

7. How will students' difficulties be recognized along the way?

We are going to have to have some pretty structured observational strategies to be sure everyone is progressing. Some of us want to administer a forced choice test mid-point and at the conclusion to be sure students are getting it. Maybe we'll do so this time to see how it works out.

8. How will assessment results be communicated to students and parents?

Portfolios! We will have students do a table of contents of their artifacts with a list of the learning standards incorporated in each artifact. We may invite parents to view the presentations – but with so many working during the day it may not be a good idea. Perhaps we can invite some other adults – the DARE officer, librarian, principal – to view the presentations.

Integrated Instructional Design

Major Learning Theme or Big Idea

Interdependence of living things and the environment.

Reading Standards/Benchmarks

1. Recognize compare/contrast text structure as embedded in informational text.
2. Recognize descriptive text structure.
3. Use context to determine word meanings: habitats, regurgitate, prey.
4. Use reference material (Internet) to obtain information.

Writing Standards/Benchmarks

1. Use report writing format to present information related to the topic of study.
2. Present information in a clear and coherent manner.
3. Use correct spelling and mechanics.
4. Use Hyper-Studio to generate report.

Listening and Speaking Standards/Benchmarks

1. Speak clearly and precisely using appropriate volume.
2. Use eye contact when speaking.
3.

Science Standards/Benchmarks

1. Wolves live in organized units.
2. Wolves have a communication system.
3. Wolves cooperate in hunting.
4. Wolves are an endangered species.
5. Wolves are part of the ecosystem of the tundra.

Physical Education Standards/Benchmarks

1.
2.   None Applicable
3.

Social Studies Standards/Benchmarks

1. Characteristics, location, and extent of the tundra
2.
3.

Fine Arts Standards/Benchmarks

1. Research artistic renderings of wolves — compare to photos of real wolves (optional)
2.
3.

Mathematics Standards/Benchmarks

1.
2.   None Applicable
3.

Figure 2.3

INTEGRATED INSTRUCTIONAL PLANNER – PART 2

LEARNING STANDARDS/BENCHMARKS (skills, concepts, strategies, processes)	OPENING ACTIVITIES	TEACHING STRATEGIES/STUDENT ACTIVITIES	STUDENT GROUPING ARRANGEMENT	MATERIALS AND RESOURCES	ASSESSMENT
Survey and predict what a reading text selection is about. Recognize text structure: (1) compare/contrast is the minor text structure of gray wolf, artic wolf, tundra wolf (2) description used as a major structure Develop vocabulary specific to a unit of study: • habitats p. 3, 14 • regurgitate p. 6 • prey p. 7, 8–9, 11 • others to be determined during class discussion	Ask about prior experiences and background knowledge of wolves. Fill in Anticipation Guide worksheet. Preview selection (Book Walk) Predict the kind of information that will be learned from reading this text.		Whole class	Test: *Call of the Wolves* (Berger) Anticipation Guide Worksheet	Observe students to determine on task behavior, level of text difficulty.
Research and organize major concepts: • wolves live in organized units • wolves have a communication system • wolves cooperate in hunting • wolves are an endangered species • wolves are part of the tundra ecosystem Organize information in report format Write to convey information (expository)		Independent reading of text. Discussion of text structure and context clues.	Individual support group for less able readers. Whole class	Text	Continue observation of students. Use observational checklist.
		Concept Mapping (after reading selection)	Small groups (jigsaw approach)	Chart paper, transparancies, markers	Student presentations of concept maps (use Speaking Rubric to assess).
		Report related to major concepts, i.e., compare and contrast wolf and human communication. Review rubric for informational reports.		Internet resources Presentation software program	Written report (use existing rubric for informational reports)
CONCLUSIONS/CONNECTIONS/REFLECTIONS • Speak clearly and distinctly to an audience • Discuss prior and newly acquired information		Revisit anticipation guide. Discuss similarities and differences to *Julie of the Wolves, Call of the Wild.*	Whole group	Discussion questions	Share reports with other classes, parents/family.

Figure 2.4

Integrated Instructional Design

PLANNING GUIDE—INTEGRATED INSTRUCTION

DESIGN

Consider these questions as a thinking guide as you plan a differentiated instructional design.

Planning Questions and Decisions	Information and Data Sources	Notes and Comments
1. What are the learning standards to be achieved?	Use the Integrated Instructional Planner, Part 1 completed in section one of this Planning Guide to document the learning standards that will be taught.	Be sure to align the learning standards to the activities as shown on the Integrated Instructional Planner. Redundancies should be noted and eliminated.
2. What is a motivating opening for the unit?		Create interest and anticipation in the unit.
3. What are some possible teaching/learning strategies?	Curriculum guides, teaching manuals, professional literature, best practices information, etc. are sources of information for teaching and learning activities.	Use the Integrated Instructional Planner, Part 2 as you consider the planning questions in column one.
4. What materials are needed to support and enhance learning?	Check the materials and resources available through the school, library, community. Students may be asked to bring in related materials if needed and if they have access to them.	
5. What is the appropriate use of technology?	Check Internet sources and software programs.	
6. How will students be grouped?		If small group instruction is planned consider how this will occur – needs based, interest based, other.
7. What opportunities will students have to reflect on their learning?		Remember to provide time for reflection and processing throughout the unit – not just at the end.
	Continued on page 58.	

LESSON DESIGN

In planning integrated instruction, appropriate teaching strategies and learning activities are developed that are directly connected to the learning standards. A single activity may incorporate several learning standards. The complexity of the activities varies with the level of maturity and capabilities of the students and the expertise and confidence of the teacher.

The Integrated Instructional Planner, Part 2 (Figure 2.4) is an overview of how the learning standards are taught. It includes a statement of the learning standards in relation to teaching strategies and student activities. The Lesson Plan Form (Figure 1.12) introduced in chapter 1 contains the components of effective lesson plans. These components are as important in planning integrated instruction as they are in planning single standard lessons. Novice teachers will find it helpful to work out more detailed plans. Experienced teachers may not need such specificity in planning. A complete overview such as that provided in the Planning Guide, however, is necessary for planning and documenting how integrated instruction is to occur.

DESIGN – INTEGRATED
Planning Questions and Decisions
Grade 5 Team

1. What are the learning standards to be achieved?
The major learning of this unit is: Interdependence of living things and the environment. The learning standards cover reading, writing, listening/speaking, science, and social studies. A fine arts objective is an included option. The Integrated Instructional Planner, Part 1 contains the specific list of all the standards.

2. What is a motivating opening for the unit?
All classes will attend the opening activity where the learning standards, purpose, and overview of activities will be described. (Parents could be invited to attend the opening.) Afterwards, students will convene in their teams to discuss what they already know about the topic and preview some of the resources they will use.

3. What are some possible teaching/learning strategies?
Cooperative activities will be balanced with independent activities. Some whole group instruction will be necessary. Guided reading strategies may be used with students who need more support.

4. What materials are needed to support and enhance learning?
Numerous trade books have been preselected and will be available for student use. Also see #6 below.

5. What is the appropriate use of technology?
Students will have opportunities to use the Internet for further research. Presentational software will be used to generate reports.

6. How will students be grouped?
There are four classrooms included in this unit. Two teachers will team teach their groups. All students will be brought together in the library for the presentations on the last three days.

7. What opportunities will students have to reflect on their learning?
Students will revisit the anticipation guide filled out at the beginning of their study of wolves. They will discuss similarities and differences of fiction and nonfiction selections on wolves.

(Continued on page 59.)

Section 2

PLANNING GUIDE—INTEGRATED INSTRUCTION (CONTINUED)
DESIGN
Use these questions to plan an integrated instructional design.

Planning Questions and Decisions	Information and Data Sources	Notes and Comments
8. What mini-lessons will be conducted?	See the Basic Lesson Plan Form (Figure 1.12)	Even when learning standards are integrated, it is necessary to develop specific lesson plans for day to day teaching. These lessons contain all the components of the Basic Lesson Design (chapter 1). • motivating opening • teaching/learning strategies • materials and resources • student groups • closure • follow up practice • assessment
9. What forms of practice will be used?		Students may be grouped to address common needs.
10. How long will this unit take?	Calendar of school events, holidays, curriculum pacing guides, and testing schedules are sources of information for scheduling.	Develop a specific organized calendar and schedule for the activites.
11. Are there any foreseeable pitfalls in this lesson?		Think ahead to avoid potential difficulties.
12. What will I do if the lesson/unit doesn't work out?		A fall-back plan is helpful to avoid potential chaos.

 Section 3

EVIDENCE OF LEARNING

The assessment of student learning is initially considered in section one of the Planning Guide for Integrated Instructional Design. When planning for the integrated unit nears completion, the assessment of student learning and expectations for performance are reconsidered and finalized. Performance assessments with clearly defined rubrics that spell out the criteria for performance and define expectations are appropriate to use with integrated lessons and units. An example of a four-point scale rubric appears in

Section 2

DESIGN
Planning Questions and Decisions (Continued)
Grade 5 Team

8. What mini-lessons will be conducted?
- *How to use presentational software (all students)*
- *Compare/contrast text structure in reading and writing (all students)*
- *Word study (group based on need)*

9. What forms of practice will be used?
Students who appear to have difficulty with reading vocabulary or report writing will be grouped together for additional support lessons relating to those skills.

10. How long will this unit take?
The study will begin on March 4 and continue for ten days. Students will work on this project for approximately two hours per day. The teachers will schedule mutually convenient times. The amount of time may vary depending on how the students progress.

11. Are there any foreseeable pitfalls in this lesson?
With all this activity going on, some students may be distracted or off-task. Also, some students may not participate fully in the cooperative groups. We'll have to monitor closely and facilitate and model appropriate learning behaviors.

12. What alternatives are there if the lesson doesn't work out?
A demonstration will be used if the student activity doesn't work out as planned. Students will observe and record their findings in their science logs.

Figure 2.5. It describes the level of performance for each of the criteria. The rubric is a tool for the teacher to use in assessing student learning and is also useful to communicate performance expectations to students and parents. Students use the rubric to plan how they will accomplish a task and to evaluate their own performance. An effective teaching/learning strategy is for students to participate in the construction of the rubric.

Integrated Instructional Design

PLANNING GUIDE—INTEGRATED INSTRUCTION

EVIDENCE OF LEARNING

Use these questions to plan an integrated instructional design.

Planning Questions and Decisions	Information and Data Sources	Notes and Comments
1. How will students demonstrate their learning?	See curriculum resource information and best practices information related to types of assessment.	Refer to your planning notes in section one as you finalize decisions regarding assessment.
2. How will the assessment be scored?	Design appropriate rubrics. Consider student participation in design of rubrics.	Possible assessments to consider for integrated learning are usually performance based.
3. How will learning be reported?	Consider the development and use of student portfolios as a means of providing feedback to students and parents.	If a schoolwide grading scale is required, be sure to align rubric levels with the grading scale.
4. How will the assessment results be used?		Use assessment results to determine student strengths and weaknesses and plan the next lessons. When school report cards are in terms of specific content areas and classroom instruction is integrated, assessments need to be correlated to specific learning objectives. The Integrated Instructional Planner (Part 1) may be used to show this correlation by adding a column for the assessments.

Section 3

EVIDENCE OF LEARNING
Planning Questions and Decisions
Grade 5 Team

1. How will the students demonstrate their learning?	2. How will the assessment be scored?	3. How will the assessment be reported?	4. How will the assessment results be used?
a. Concept Map related to wolves (group task) b. Concept Map presentation to class (all members of group will have a part) c. Written reflection by each student on their participation in the group's work.	a. Develop rubric for concept map activity. Distribute to students when assignment is given. b. Speaking/Listening rubric to assess presentation of information. c. No scoring – comments only.	a. Group scores based on rubric. b. Individual scores based on rubric. c. Comments from the teacher.	a. Feedback for students on their work as a group. b. Feedback for students and teacher on how speaking/listening skills are used. c. Feedback for teacher on how students participated in the group work.
Selected response test (20 items)	Answer key (20 items, 5 points each); Sign up to use scantron for scoring.	Go over test items with students. Grades will be determined according to the schoolwide grading scale.	Determine which students need reinforcement of factual information. Students make corrections as necessary. Include results in quarterly report card grade.
Written report – specific topic related to wolves selected by each student.	Writing rubric (district)	Copy of rubric showing performance level will be returned to students. Teacher comments will be included as appropriate.	The rubric will provide feedback to the student. A total of 10 points for this assignment will be included in the quarterly report card grade.
Report – group task. Students will use information from their individual reports to create a computer generated presentation.	Rubric on presentation of reports	Copy of rubric for each group will be scored. Teacher comments will be included.	Feedback for students and teacher on how students worked as a group.
Portfolios – All assessments above will be included with an explanation of the learning standards included in each one.	Rubric developed by teacher and students.	Students will share portfolios with parents.	Feedback for students, teachers, and parents on group and individual participation in this unit.

Integrated Instructional Design

SCORING RUBRIC FOR A STORY MAP	ATTEMPTED (1)	DEVELOPING (2)	DEVELOPED (3)	ACCOMPLISHED (4)
SETTING	Shows no evidence of understanding time or place.	Identifies a time and place.	Identifies time and place and provides some description.	Identifies detailed componenets of time and place with extensive description.
CHARACTERS	Does not identify characters or incorrectly lists characters.	Lists some characters. May provide limited description.	Lists main characters and included some roles, traits, and/or relationships.	Identifies all main charactiers; clearly defines their roles, traits, and/or relationships.
PROBLEM	Identifies incorrect problem.	Shows limited or incomplete understanding of the problem.	States the main problem clearly.	States the problem completely and elaborates reasons, background, etc.
EVENTS	Lists incorrect events.	States some major events.	States major events in proper sequence.	States all major events clearly and in proper sequence with some elaboration.
SOLUTION	Identifies incorrect solution.	Identifies partial solution.	States the solution clearly.	States the solutions clearly and explains why it resolves the problem.
PERSONAL REACTION	Does not provide any personal reaction or connection to prior knowledge.	Provides very limited personal reaction.	Provides personal reaction and explains some connections to prior knowledge and other learning.	Personal reaction and connections are logically explained.

Figure 2.5

USING THE INTEGRATED INSTRUCTIONAL DESIGN PLANNING GUIDE

The Integrated Instructional Design Planning Guide is a thinking process approach to planning instruction. Preservice teachers and novice teachers will find it helpful to follow the all the steps in using the planning guide. Teachers who have little or no previous experience in planning integrated instruction will find the planning guide a supportive scaffold in their initial efforts. As a result, subsequent planning will be easier. Experienced teachers with an understanding of instructional design may find that they need only review the questions and activities and focus on those areas that will enhance their planning efforts. An example of how a fifth-grade teaching team completed the Planning Guide was shown. The team used the guide to structure their discussion and begin their planning.

1. Read the planning guide in its entirety

Become familiar with the planning guide before you begin using it. This will save you time in the long run. Get the "big picture" in mind before filling in the details.

2. Think it through

Begin with Section 1: Desired Results. Think about the questions in column one and write down your thoughts and reactions to the planning questions. Consult the data and information sources suggested in column two and note the reminders and supplemental information in column three. Add notes and comments of your own that will be helpful in subsequent planning. Planning questions may be deleted or added to fit your situation. Continue through Section 2: Lesson Design and Section 3: Evidence of Learning.

3. Synthesize information

Step two above has led you to study and analyze the current curriculum and begin planning integrated instruction. The information you have obtained is now synthesized and translated onto the Integrated Instructional Planner

# Integrated Instructional Design

(Figures 2.3 and 2.4). Part two of the planner follows the same general format and contains the same general components as the Basic Lesson Design Planner (chapter 1). Any section of the Integrated Planner (Part 2) can be detailed further on the Lesson Plan form presented in chapter one.

SUMMARY OF GENERAL PLANNING STEPS FOR INTEGRATED LEARNING

The Integrated Instructional Design Planning Guide contains the detailed description of how to plan for integrated instruction. The steps below are a general outline of the process. (See the Blackline section of this chapter.)

1. Think through the process of integrated instruction using the Integrated Instructional Design Planning Guide.
2. Determine rationale for using an integrated learning approach.
3. Discuss and select an integration model. (Figure 2.2)
4. Develop a Curriculum Calendar Map.
5. Align topics of study on the Curriculum Calendar Map.
6. Document learning standards and connections on the Integrated Instructional Planner, Part 1.
7. Develop the instructional overview (For Integrated Instructional Planner). Determine and develop specific lesson plans as needed (see chapter one, Figure 1.12).

REFLECTIVE PRACTICE

Merely following an outline or filling in a template is not sufficient to develop expertise in planning powerful lessons. Planning is a metacognitive, reflective process where the teacher thinks, reflects, adjusts, redirects, fiddles, and fine-tunes the various components until a powerful lesson emerges. When reflection is an intrinsic part of the instructional planning process and teachers take time to analyze their planning efforts, they learn through their experiences, and future planning becomes more effective and efficient.

What Costa (1991) called "inner dialogue" is essential to professional growth, change, and improvement. Use the Inner Dialogue page to reflect on planning actions, attempts, and results of using the Integrated Instructional Design. Be open-minded but skeptical. Consider pros and cons, benefits, and challenges. Look beyond what was accomplished to why and how it was accomplished.

Integrated Instructional Design

INNER DIALOGUE

Take time to reflect on the process you have gone through to plan integrated instruction. Keep in mind that you are developing planning skills that will become stronger with experience and practice. As with all learning, reflecting on your experience will deepen your understanding. At some point, you will feel comfortable taking some short cuts and you will understand why and how you are able to do so. Keep your notes and refer to them when you plan again.

Fact This is what I did in the planning process.	**React** This is what I think about it and how I might change or modify it.
Some new learning	
Some benefits	
Some challenges	

Monday 10/2	Tuesday 10/3	Wednesday 10/4		Thursday 10/5	Friday 10/6	Notes
		Group Presentations →		8:15—9:05 Use attentive listening w/read aloud (SSR)	State testing	Schedule Conferences
8:15—9:05 Assign Eaten for silent reading	Group Presentations Assign A.W.					
9:10—10:00 Organize Coop groups	Specials Math Committee Meeting	Graph results of survey (pictograph) →		9:10—10:00 Specials P.E.	↓ →	
12:05—12:55 Guest panel for PBL examination Assign A.W.	Guest panel for PBL examination Assign A.W.	Role Play Group 1—Sc. 1 Group 2—Sc. 2		10:05—10:55 Eaten fal reports (SSR)		→
1:00—1:50 Supervision	L U	N →		1:00—1:50 Supervision	L U N C H	
1:55—12:45 Specials	Class disc. conflict and feelings in lit. Assign A.W.	Specials →		1:55—12:45 • Collage • move to assigned centers (SSR)	Specials →	
12:50—1:40 Staff Meeting Assign proj. for next mo.	Lab time Use Internet sources	Bridging snapshots to explain scientific process →		12:50—1:40 Turn in Community survey materials (SSR)	State testing ↓	
1:40—2:35 Group Presentations	Begin to formulate/create mobiles Assign A.W.	Cont: wk on mobiles—Each group Give prog. report		1:40—2:35 Re-group/move seats (SSR)		

Integrated Instructional Design

CURRICULUM CALENDAR MAP

	Language Arts	Social Studies	Science	Mathematics	Music	Art	Phys. Ed.
September							
October							
November							
December							
January							
February							
March							
April							
May							

SkyLight Professional Development

Section 1

DESIRED RESULTS – INTEGRATED
Planning Questions and Decisions

1. How and why will teaching and learning be more effective if learning standards are integrated within lessons rather than taught separately?

2. What connections exist among the learning standards?

3. How will learning standards be organized and documented?

4. What standards are a higher priority than others?

5. How will the learning standards be assessed? (Are combined or embedded assessments feasible?)

6. What assessment materials are available and what materials need to be developed?

7. How will students' difficulties be recognized along the way?

8. How will assessment results be communicated to students and parents?

Section 2

DESIGN – INTEGRATED
Planning Questions and Decisions

1. What are the learning standards to be achieved?

2. What is a motivating opening for the unit?

3. What are some possible teaching/learning strategies?

4. What materials are needed to support and enhance learning?

5. What is the appropriate use of technology?

6. How will students be grouped?

7. What opportunities will students have to reflect on their learning?

8. What mini-lessons will be conducted?

9. What forms of practice will be used?

10. How long will this unit take?

11. Are there any foreseeable pitfalls in this lesson?

12. What will I do if the lesson/unit doesn't work out?

Section 3

EVIDENCE OF LEARNING – INTEGRATED
Planning Questions and Decisions

1. How will students demonstrate their learning?

2. How will the assessment be scored?

3. How will learning be reported?

4. How will the assessment results be used?

Integrated Instructional Design

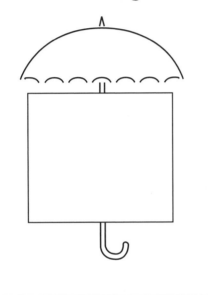

Major Learning Theme or Big Idea

Reading Standards/Benchmarks
1.
2.
3.
4.

Writing Standards/Benchmarks
1.
2.
3.
4.

Listening/Speaking Standards/Benchmarks
1.
2.
3.

Science Standards/Benchmarks
1.
2.
3.

Physical Education Standards/ Benchmarks
1.
2.
3.

Social Studies Standards/Benchmarks
1.
2.
3.

Fine Arts Standards/Benchmarks
1.
2.
3.

Mathematics Standards/Benchmarks
1.
2.
3.

Integrated Instructional Planner – Part 2						
Learning Standards/Benchmarks (skills, concepts, strategies, processes)	Opening Activities	Teaching Strategies/Student Activities	Student Grouping Arrangement	Materials and Resources	Assessment	
Conclusions/Connections/Reflections						

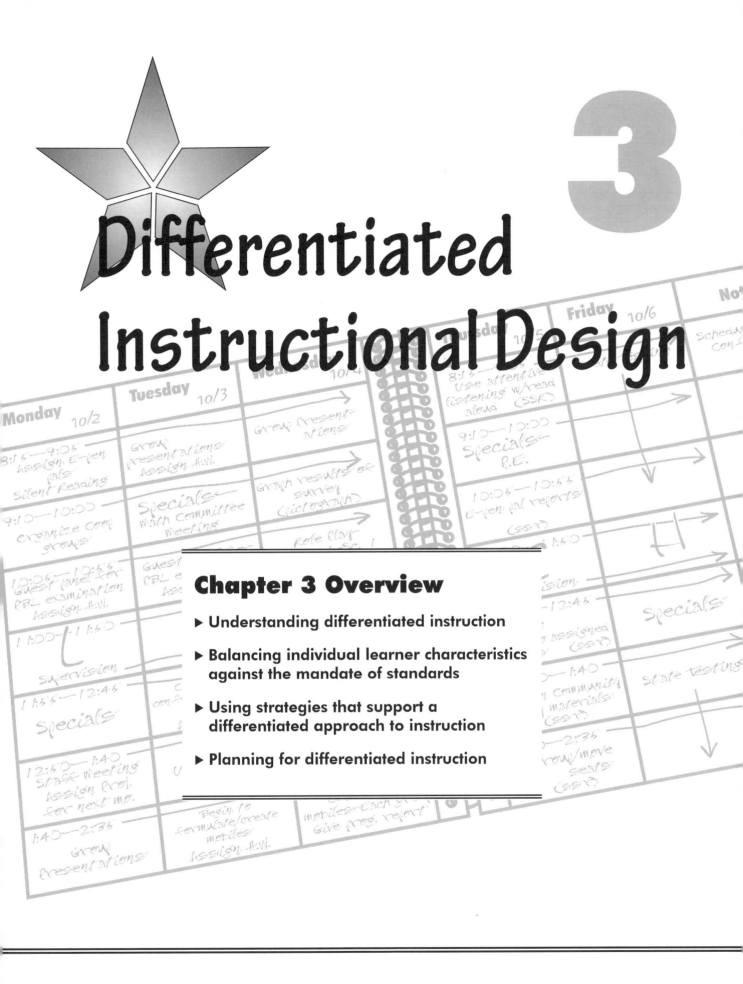

Differentiated Instructional Design

Chapter 3 Overview

▶ **Understanding differentiated instruction**

▶ **Balancing individual learner characteristics against the mandate of standards**

▶ **Using strategies that support a differentiated approach to instruction**

▶ **Planning for differentiated instruction**

Differentiated Instructional Design

Anyone who spends even a short time in a classroom sees that students differ not only in physical appearance but also in how they learn, what their interests are, the prior experiences they have had, and their cognitive strengths and weaknesses. These differences become even more pronounced as students advance through the grades. A "one-size-fits-all" model of instruction, therefore, cannot possibly reach all students in a classroom. "That students differ may be inconvenient, but it is inescapable" (Sizer 1999).

None of us is quite like another,
None of us is quite the same,
Each of us is like no other,
Each of us is not the same.

Differentiated instruction as it is practiced today differs from past approaches that attempted to reduce the range of student differences through pull-out programs, ability grouping, tracking, and retention. These approaches sorted students according to ability with usually no accommodation for how they learned. Generally, lower ability students were taught with lower level textbooks and materials, and higher ability students were taught with higher level textbooks and materials. Research on ability grouping programs has been generally unfavorable (Slavin 1987; Oakes 1988; Zemelman, Daniels, and Hyde 1993; Good and Brophy 1997). Differentiated instruction as it practiced today is quite different from past approaches.

THE MANY FACETS OF DIFFERENTIATED INSTRUCTION

Differentiated instruction is a teaching approach that provides a variety of learning options to accommodate differences in how students learn. Some differences that impact learning are related to the student's prior knowledge and experience, learning preferences and modality, cognitive level, and personal interests. According to Csikszentmihalyi (1990), a learner reaches his or her fullest capacity when a task is at an optimal level—neither too difficult nor too simple. When the learner's mental and emotional focus are linked together in learning, a state of "flow" occurs that enhances and sustains learning (Goleman 1995). It is this state of flow that teachers try to create for their students by providing appropriately challenging activities.

Instructional Needs

Instructional needs are determined by assessing what a student knows and is able to do in relation to a learning standard. A learning profile obtained through various assessments points to skills, concepts, and/or processes that need to be further developed. Assessment sources may include observation of classroom performance, evaluation of artifacts (the work the student produces), performance-based assessments, and standardized test results.

Multiple Intelligences

Consideration of instructional needs alone, however, does not give us all the information necessary from which to develop instructional activities. Effective instruction combines what students learn with how they learn. In the past we examined I.Q. in an attempt to determine the strength of a student's ability to learn. In *Frames of Mind,* Howard Gardner questions the view of I.Q. as a single entity and theorizes the existence of several intellectual strengths or competences within an individual (1983). Gardner recognizes eight intelligences, which are briefly described in Figure 3.1. This summary should not be considered as a complete description of Gardner's theory, which is far more complex than what is outlined here. For a complete discussion of Gardner's theory see *Frames of Mind* (1983).

Students who have a proclivity toward one of these "intelligences" will feel comfortable and confident when participating in activities that involve its use. Therefore, it makes sense to provide students with activities that will allow them to use their preferred intelligence to perform at their best.

GARDNER'S INTELLIGENCES

Verbal/Linguistic: The ability to use with clarity the core operations of language.

Musical/Rhythmic: The ability to use the core set of musical elements.

Logical/Mathematical: The ability to use inductive and deductive reasoning, solve abstract problems, and understand complex relationships.

Visual/Spatial: The ability to perceive the visual world accurately and recreate one's visual experiences.

Naturalist: The ability to survive in and adapt to one's own environment by understanding nature and all of its elements.

Bodily/Kinesthetic: The ability to control and interpret body motions, manipulate physical objects, and establish harmony between the body and mind.

Interpersonal: The ability to get along with, interact with, work with, and motivate others toward a common goal.

Intrapersonal: The ability to form an accurate model of oneself and to use that model to operate effectively in life.

Figure 3.1

Differentiated Instructional Design

Learning Modalities

We have long known that learning modalities—auditory, visual, kinesthetic, and tactile—influence how we learn. Simply put, visual learners benefit from graphic representations, auditory learners benefit from aural representations, kinesthetic learners benefit from bodily involvement activities, and tactile learners benefit from touching and feeling shapes, forms, and textures (Sprenger 1999). Teachers routinely use visual aids such as posters, charts, and models to accompany lessons. They capitalize on student's auditory strengths through auditory input of recordings, "talking toys," conversation, discussion, songs, and dialogue. They provide activities in which students build or construct a physical representation of something they are learning about, i.e., water cycle, bridges, story elements, skeletal system. They provide movement activities that depict some idea or concept such as a dance or physical movement to reinforce multiplication facts. An individual's predominant learning modality does not negate the presence of the other modalities. For this reason, teachers find it beneficial to provide multimodal activities throughout their lessons.

> An individual's predominant learning modality does not negate the presence of the other modalities.

Cognitive Levels

Learners engage in types of thinking that range from a simple literal level to more complex abstract levels (Bloom 1984). These levels are not distinct but overlap and are used simultaneously by students in learning situations (Good and Brophy 1997). All students need and benefit from learning activities that challenge them to use complex thinking and reasoning.

Background of Experiences

Students who have a rich background of experiences and are able to connect new experiences into patterns of meaning seem to learn and retain concepts better than those who do not (Caine and Caine 1991; Jensen 2000). Teachers help students to make sense of learning by connecting new learning to what is already known. When students know very little about a topic, it is important to build the background that will enable them to benefit from instruction. When students have extensive knowledge of a topic, instruction should enrich and extend what they already know.

Personal Interests

Students develop an interest in a particular topic or area for a variety of reasons. Some interests are fleeting, some last a lifetime. Regardless of what or why, interests do motivate and sustain learning. The teacher who allows students choices and opportunities to select learning activities capitalizes on personal interests that lead students into learning and studying a topic (Diamond and Hopson 1998).

The Differentiated Classroom

A differentiated instructional design may be used for a part of the school year for certain units or it may become an overarching philosophy toward which all classroom instruction is geared. Tomlinson (1999) describes the principles of a "differentiated classroom" that are more extensive than differentiation as an instructional approach. These principles go beyond instructional differentiation to include beliefs and practices that may well apply to other instructional approaches as well (see Figure 3.2).

The associated planning and teaching techniques incorporated in differentiated instructional design evolve as teachers become experienced and comfortable with this approach. Teachers who use differentiated instruction generally begin by implementing short units, which are modified and expanded over time. Planning differentiated instruction coordinates student learning characteristics (how students learn) with learning standards (what students learn). Darling-Hammond (1997, 74) states, "...there is no prepackaged set of steps or lessons that will secure understanding for every learner in the same way." Research supports teaching practices that honor the individuality of students in terms of their experiences, interests, and prior knowledge.

> Teachers who use differentiated instruction generally begin by implementing short units, which are modified and expanded over time.

Differentiated Instructional Design

TOMLINSON'S PRINCIPLES FOR THE DIFFERENTIATED CLASSROOM

The teacher focuses on the essentials.
The teacher selects and teaches the concepts, skills, and principles that are essential in each subject area. The teacher has a clear sense of what is to be accomplished and conveys this sense to his or her students.

The teacher attends to student differences.
The teacher is aware of the differences as well as the commonalities of his or her students and plans instruction to capitalize on both. Diversity is acknowledged and valued.

Assessment and instruction are inseparable.
Assessment in differentiated classrooms provides diagnostic information to both the teacher and the students on progress toward specific goals. Assessment information is used to plan subsequent instruction.

The teacher modifies content, process, and products.
Modifications made through differentiation address the content of learning, learning skills and processes, and the tasks students engage in to produce evidence of their learning. Differentiated classrooms include whole class, nondifferentiated instruction along with differentiated learning opportunities. Students participate as members within the whole learning community.

All students participate in respectful work.
The teacher in a differentiated classroom shows respect for the similarities as well as differences in students and offers all students opportunities to be involved in interesting, important, and engaging work.

The teacher and students collaborate in learning.
A differentiated classroom is student centered. Students participate in the governance of the classroom and have responsibility for its management. The teacher facilitates learning activities through motivation, guidance, and feedback. Learning is the "work" of the classroom.

The teacher balances group and individual norms.
The teacher understands student progress in terms of individual growth as well as growth measured according to group norms. The teacher helps all students realize their individual potential whether a given student is below or beyond grade level expectations.

The teacher and students work together flexibly.
Instructional strategies, activities, materials, pacing, and grouping are planned to accommodate students' differences for optimal learning. Grouping arrangements are varied and flexible.

Adapted for *The Differentiated Classroom* by Carol Ann Tomlinson. © 1999 by ASCD. Used with permission of ASCD, Alexandria, VA.

Figure 3.2

WHY DIFFERENTIATED INSTRUCTION IS A GOOD IDEA

Support for differentiated instruction is seen in recent research on how the brain learns. While brain research in itself does not tell us how to teach, it can inform our instructional practices. Jensen (2000) says that the right amount of challenge is a critical element in learning—too much leads to frustration, too little leads to boredom. If students in a classroom are all expected to perform the same learning activity, it is likely that some will be frustrated and some will be bored because the level of challenge does not meet their needs. A differentiated instructional plan helps to ensure that students participate in learning activities that are at (or at least close to) their optimal learning level.

When students are engaged and challenged in their work, they become motivated and invested in their learning.

Activities that help students see connections to real-life situations and apply what they learn to new situations create opportunities for transfer of learning (Fogarty 1997). Transfer, or use of knowledge, skills, and processes in new situations, is perhaps the ultimate goal of education. It matters little if we possess vast amounts of knowledge and information if we cannot use and apply that knowledge.

Students need complex real-life experiences to learn and grow. Simple linear approaches such as those designed to teach isolated skills are not as powerful as those that provide interactive, hands-on activities where students explore, manipulate, and connect ideas and concepts (Caine and Caine 1991). An example of a complex activity that asks students to apply what they know to solve a problem or perform a task is shown in Figure 3.3. The student must first conceptualize what he or she is to do or, in other words, determine what the problem is. He or she must then call to mind which skills and processes already learned will help solve the problem. Working through the task, the student continually evaluates whether or not he or she is on the right track and makes adjustments accordingly. This metacognitive

Working through the task, the student continually evaluates whether or not he or she is on the right track and makes adjustments accordingly.

DESIGN A COMPACT DISC COVER

A famous compact disc company has asked you to design a compact disc cover. You are to submit your design on graph paper according to the company's directions that are outlined below. Be sure you include all the necessary items.

1. The title should occupy one quarter of the cover.

2. Include all of the following items on the cover and tell what fractional part of the cover each occupies:
   • titles and descriptions of songs
   • information about the artist
   • pictures or graphics

3. Explain in words what fractional part each item is compared to the whole cover.

Figure 3.3

Differentiated Instructional Design

ILLINOIS STATE STANDARDS FOR LEARNING

State Goal 1: READ WITH UNDERSTANDING AND FLUENCY.
Why This Goal Is Important: Reading is essential. It is the process by which people gain information and ideas from books, newspapers, manuals, letters, contracts, advertisements, and a host of other materials. Using strategies for constructing meaning before, during, and after reading will help students connect what they read now with what they have learned in the past. Students who read well and widely build a strong foundation for learning in all areas of life.

Standard A. Apply word analysis and vocabulary skills to comprehend selections.

EARLY ELEMENTARY	LATE ELEMENTARY	MIDDLE/JUNIOR HIGH SCHOOL	EARLY HIGH SCHOOL	LATE HIGH SCHOOL
1.A.1a Apply word analysis skills e.g., phonics, (word patterns) to recognize new words.	**1.A.2a** Read and comprehend unfamiliar words using root words, synonyms, antonyms, word origins, and derivations.	**1.A.3a** Apply knowledge of word origins and derivations to comprehend words used in specific content areas (e.g., scientific political, literary, mathematical).	**1.A.4a** Expand knowledge of word origins and derivations and use idioms, analogies, metaphors, and similies to extend vocabulary development.	**1.A.5a** Identify and analyze new terminology applying knowledge of word origins and derivations in a variety of practical settings.
1.A.1b Comprehend unfamiliar words using context clues and prior knowledge; verify meanings with resource materials.	**1.A.2b** Clarify word meaning using context clues and a variety of resources including glossaries, dictionaries, and thesauruses.	**1.A.3b** Analyze the meaning of words and phrases in their context.	**1.A.4b** Analyze the meaning of words and phrases and use analogies to explain the relationships among them.	**1.A.5b** Analyze the meaning of abstract concepts and the effects of particular word and phrase choices.

Figure 3.4

strategy is critical in problem solving and increases the likelihood of accuracy. The solution—the outcome of the task—is judged against some criteria (either provided by the teacher or determined by the student).

THE ROLE OF LEARNING STANDARDS IN DIFFERENTIATED INSTRUCTION

Learning standards provide descriptions of what students should know and be able to do. There is no lack of learning standard information available today: most state boards of education, professional organizations, and school

ILLINOIS STATE STANDARDS FOR LEARNING

Standard B. Apply reading strategies to improve understanding and fluency.

EARLY ELEMENTARY	LATE ELEMENTARY	MIDDLE/JUNIOR HIGH SCHOOL	EARLY HIGH SCHOOL	LATE HIGH SCHOOL
1.B.1a Establish purposes for reading, make predictions, connect important ideas, and link text to previous experiences and knowledge.	**1.B.2a** Establish purposes for reading; survey materials; ask questions; make predictions; connect, clarify, and extend ideas.	**1.B.3a** Preview reading materials, make predictions, and relate reading to information from other sources.	**1.B.4a** Preview reading materials, clarify meaning, analyze overall themes and coherence, and relate reading with information from other sources.	**1.B.5a** Relate reading to prior knowledge and experience and make connections to related information.
1.B.1b Identify genres (forms and purposes) of fiction, nonfiction, poetry, and electronic literary forms.	**1.B.2b** Identify structure (e.g., description, compare/contrast, cause and effect, sequence) of nonfiction texts to improve comprehension.	**1.B.3b** Identify text structure and create a visual representation (e.g., graphic organizer, outline, drawing) to use while reading.	**1.B.4b** Analyze, interpret, and compare a variety of texts for purpose, structure, content, detail, and effect.	**1.B.5b** Analyze the defining characteristics and structures of a variety of complex literary genres and describe how genre affects the meaning and function of the texts.
1.B.1c Continuously check and clarify for understanding (e.g., reread, read ahead, use visual and context clues, ask questions, retell, use meaningful substitutions).	**1.B.2c** Continuously check and clarify for understanding (e.g., in addition to previous skills, clarify terminology, seek additional information).	**1.B.3c** Continuously check and clarify for understanding (e.g., in addition to previous skills, draw comparisons to other readings).	**1.B.4c** Read age-appropriate material with fluency and accuracy.	**1.B.5c** Evaluate a variety of compositions for purpose, structure, content, and details for use in school or at work.
1.B.1d Read age-appropriate material aloud with fluency and accuracy.	**1.B.2d** Read age-appropriate material aloud with fluency and accuracy.	**1.B.3d** Read age-appropriate material with fluency and accuracy.		**1.B.5d** Read age-appropriate material with fluency and accuracy.

Figure 3.4, continued

districts have developed lists of content area standards. The formats used by different organizations may be different, but the purpose and intent is the same—to provide information on what students should know and be able to do. An example of the Illinois State Learning Standards for Language Arts

Differentiated Instructional Design

ILLINOIS STATE STANDARDS FOR LEARNING

Standard C. Comprehend a broad range of reading materials.

EARLY ELEMENTARY	LATE ELEMENTARY	MIDDLE/JUNIOR HIGH SCHOOL	EARLY HIGH SCHOOL	LATE HIGH SCHOOL
1.C.1a Use information to form questions and verify predictions.	**1.C.2a** Use information to form and refine questions and predictions.	**1.C.3a** Use information to form, explain, and support questions and predictions.	**1.C.4a** Use questions and predictions to guide reading.	**1.C.5a** Use questions and predictions to guide reading across complex materials.
1.C.1b Identify important themes and topics.	**1.C.2b** Make and support inferences and form interpretations about main themes and topics.	**1.C.3b** Interpret and analyze entire narrative text using story elements, point of view, and theme.	**1.C.4b** Explain and justify an interpretation of a text.	**1.C.5b** Analyze and defend an interpretation of a text.
1.C.1c Make comparisons across reading selections.	**1.C.2c** Compare and contrast the content and organization of selections.	**1.C.3c** Compare, contrast, and evaluate ideas and information from various sources and genres.	**1.C.4c** Interpret, evaluate, and apply information from a variety of sources to other situations (e.g., academic, vocational, technical, personal).	**1.C.5c** Critically evaluate information from multiple sources.
1.C.1d Summarize content of reading material using text organization (e.g., story, sequence).	**1.C.2d** Summarize and make generalizations from content and relate to purpose of material.	**1.C.3d** Summarize and make generalizations from content and relate them to the purpose of the material.	**1.C.4d** Summarize and make generalizations from content and relate them to the purpose of the material.	**1.C.5d** Summarize and make generalizations from content and relate them to the purpose of the material.

Figure 3.4, continued

Goal 1: Read with Understanding and Fluency is shown in Figure 3.4. This particular example shows the standards that address the overarching goal: Read with understanding and fluency. Each of these standards is further defined as benchmarks for performance in early elementary, late elementary, middle/junior high school, early high school, and late high school. A sequence and continuity of the benchmarks stretches across the grades.

While the abundance of standards may seem to make planning an overwhelming task, a closer look reveals similarities and overlapping among the

ILLINOIS STATE STANDARDS FOR LEARNING

Standard C. Comprehend a broad range of reading materials. (cont'd)

EARLY ELEMENTARY	LATE ELEMENTARY	MIDDLE/JUNIOR HIGH SCHOOL	EARLY HIGH SCHOOL	LATE HIGH SCHOOL
1.C.1e Identify how authors and illustrators express their ideas in text and graphics (e.g., dialogue, conflict, shape, color, characters).	**1.C.2e** Explain how authors and illustrators use text and art to express their ideas (e.g., points of view, design, hues, metaphor).	**1.C.3e** Compare how authors and illustrators use text and art across materials to express their ideas (e.g., foreshadowing, flashbacks, color, strong verbs, language that inspires).	**1.C.4e** Analyze how authors and illustrators use text and art to express and emphasize their ideas (e.g., imagery, multiple points of view).	**1.C.5e** Evaluate how authors and illustrators use text and art across materials to express their ideas (e.g., complex dialogue, persuasive techniques).
1.C.1f Use information presented in simple tables, maps, and charts to form an interpretation.	**1.C.2f** Connect information presented in tables, maps, and charts to printed or electronic text.	**1.C.3f** Interpret tables that display textual information and data in visual formats.	**1.C.4f** Interpret tables, graphs, and maps in conjuction with related text.	**1.C.5f** Use tables, graphs, and maps to challenge arguments, defend conclusions, and persuade others.

Figure 3.4, continued

standards. When teachers put learning standards to use in planning instruction, they select the standards their students need to meet. Then they plan instruction focused on those standards.

In a differentiated classroom, students are not learning different things—they are learning the same things differently. Learning standards drive the development of learning activities. However, instead of a single activity all students are expected to engage in, a range of activities is offered. Even as students are involved in different learning activities, they are still addressing the same learning standards. The challenge to the teacher is to know the learning characteristics of each of his or her students and plan instruction for optimal learning. Obviously, not all differences in these characteristics can be addressed in all lessons all the time. The teacher selects the characteristics that are to be differentiated based on his or her knowledge of the students in relation to the learning standards that are to be taught. This becomes the framework for designing activities that focus on the range of differences.

Standards are central to instructional planning. Inexperienced teachers tend to jump in and begin planning activities—what the students will do. However, before planning the activities, decisions must be made regarding what students will learn—what learning standards are to be addressed. The activities are the means to this end. Tomlinson (1999) states that all students need the same essential principles and even the same key skills. The way they go about acquiring these principles and skills through various learning activities is what differentiated learning is all about. In planning differentiated instruction, the teacher must first decide what learning standards will be addressed and assessed, next decide the basis for differentiation, and then plan appropriate activities.

TEACHING WITH A DIFFERENTIATED APPROACH

Several teaching strategies lend themselves to differentiated instruction. Students may be arranged in small groups some of the time and engage in individual activities at other times. Whole group instruction may be appropriate when common instructional needs arise. A variety of materials and sources of information is necessary in differentiated classrooms. With today's easy access to information, these are easier to obtain than in the past. Examples of specific strategies that lend themselves to differentiated instruction are described below.

Cooperative Learning

Robert Sylwester (1995) discusses the importance of social interaction in learning. He believes cooperative grouping arrangements that promote positive social interaction among students enhance learning. Jensen (2000) concurs that interactions and social status affect hormone levels that may impact learning. When students work as members of a group, each contributes to the purpose of the group. The interdependence of the group members impacts the functioning of the group as well as the outcome.

In their book on best practices, Zemelman, Daniels, and Hyde (1993, 143) state that "...every child needn't study every possible topic, and that not everyone has to study all the same topics. Indeed, it is good educational practice (and solid preparation for adult life) to be part of a community where tasks and topics are parceled out to work groups, task forces, teams, or committees." Teachers may "jigsaw" an activity or task into several parts. Groups of students engage in one of the parts and then bring their learning back to the entire group. In this manner, the pieces of the jigsaw puzzle are fit together and students learn from one another.

Individual Learning (Self-Selection/Self-Pacing)

Not all classroom activities must be cooperative grouping arrangements. Just as there are valid reasons for cooperative group activities and whole group instruction, there are times when students should be allowed to work individually. A student who exhibits an intense interest in exploring a topic from another perspective, has a specialized need that does not "fit" any of the group activities, or simply prefers to work alone should be allowed to do so. Further, all students should be given opportunities to work independently to practice self-reliance and show what they can do on their own. At other times, choice of working with a group or individually gives students control over how they learn and promotes motivation and independence. All these arrangements have a place in the differentiated classroom.

Learning Centers

Materials and resources are important components for learning. A differentiated learning environment calls for a greater range of materials, since students perform different tasks and engage in different activities. Learning centers where materials are assembled for students to complete their learning activities may be set up throughout the classroom. The learning centers coincide with the task. An example of a learning center is a science experiment students perform and write up. (At the middle and high school, these are referred to as "labs" and the write-up is the lab report.) Here all the necessary materials are provided, students are given directions, and the teacher monitors and observes the students. At the kindergarten level, learning centers may be set up for students based on a particular learning standard such as letter identification. A center of this type may contain plastic letters and cards for matching, paper and pencil for tracing and writing, picture books for reading, and games for practicing letter recognition. Learning center activities may be designed for small group, partner, or individual learning.

Technology Tools

Providing materials for differentiated learning is easier today than ever before. The Internet can serve as a source of boundless content information. Several Web sites allow students to explore topics on many levels of understanding from the simple to abstract. A good starting point is http://www. britannica.com, which has links to related and rated Web sites.

Software programs are available that provide instruction on basic literal factual information (math facts) as well as more analytical, open-ended explorations of topics. Software reviews and other valuable educational technology information may be found at www.techlearning.com.

It is becoming increasingly common for students to use technology for learning and to exhibit their learning through technology. Students are able to design simple to sophisticated multimedia programs using presentational software programs. As early as second grade, students may use word processing to create stories.

TEXTBOOKS AND DIFFERENTIATED INSTRUCTION

A textbook is a teaching tool. Although common in the past, the use of a single basal text is no longer sufficient for today's student. Now more than ever before, learning to access, use, and evaluate information is a vital skill. Confining students to a single text limits their perspective. Even at an early age, students must understand that information comes from a variety of sources. A textbook is one resource to use along with other print materials, Web sites, video documents, primary source documents, expert interviews, etc.

A criticism of American education is that it promotes superficial coverage of a vast amount of material with little opportunity for deep understanding to develop (Stigler and Hiebert 1999). The volume of material contained in most textbooks and curriculum guides makes for a rushed and hurried coverage of content with little time to discuss and connect concepts. When teachers use the learning standards to sort out what is important for students to learn, they may find that not all the content contained in a textbook is necessary. They may also find that the textbook does not contain the material needed to meet the learning standards. Planning for differentiated instruction involves analyzing the materials available for learning and making choices as to what is necessary and what is not.

Beginning teachers usually feel more comfortable having the structure of a textbook to lean on. A textbook may provide resource information from which to obtain ideas on teaching strategies and student activities. Even beginning teachers, however, should use a variety of information sources in their planning and teaching.

PLANNING FOR SUCCESS IN DIFFERENTIATED INSTRUCTION

Differentiating instruction within a heterogeneous classroom requires precise planning, skillful execution, and detailed follow-up. It is a challenge to accommodate diverse student needs and maintain a realistic, manageable plan of instruction. Good and Brophy (1997) state that the effectiveness of a differentiated instructional approach is directly related to the teacher's managerial skills. An organized instructional plan is the first step to creating a productive, stimulating classroom environment. Is it realistic to assume the teacher will meet every need of every student? Probably not, but we can get a lot closer with differentiated instruction than with a "one size fits all" model. There may be one destination, but there are surely many paths.

APPLYING INSTRUCTIONAL DESIGN TO DIFFERENTIATED INSTRUCTION

Tomlinson (1999) discusses tiered activities for differentiation where the same essential learning standards are the basis for planning activities that accommodate different levels of complexity, abstractness, and open-endedness. After deciding the basis for differentiation and creating an activity that will lead to a high degree of understanding, Tomlinson recommends "cloning" that activity to produce activities of greater and lesser levels of complexity.

A matrix for unit development designed by James Curry and John Samara (1995) coordinates a modification of Bloom's cognitive levels with core subject matter and student products. The Curry/Samara Model is used to balance factual subject matter with real-world concepts, basic levels of thinking with abstract levels of thinking, and student products that range from simple to complex. The lessons developed through use of the Curry/Samara Model help teachers differentiate instruction for a wide range of learners.

The Differentiated Instructional Design Matrix (Figure 3.5) presented in this chapter is an approach to developing differentiated activities for students. The purpose is to meet a wide range of student needs related to specific learning standards.

Some learning standards require the student to know certain information or facts. Other learning standards require students to extend, perform, or apply their learning. Learning activities must be designed to meet the requirement inherent in each learning standard. The way in which the teacher designs a learning activity determines the focus and direction for students. Teachers focus and direct students through activities that are literal, relational, transformational, and extensional. Literal activities are used to

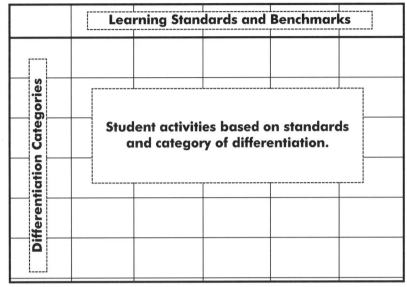

Learning Standards and Benchmarks

Differentiation Categories

Student activities based on standards and category of differentiation.

Figure 3.5

acquire basic information. Relational activities are used to connect information from various sources, including personal background knowledge. Transformational activities are used to manipulate, transcribe, or apply learning in a different way. And extensional activities are used to create, originate, evaluate, and in other ways produce something new.

In designing learning activities, the teacher uses certain words or phrases that support the requirement inherent in the learning standard. (See Designing Learning Activities Figure 1.6 for commonly used terms in planning literal, relational, transformational, and extensional learning activities.) Teachers must be cognizant that the learning standards apply to all students. All students, regardless of instructional level, need opportunities to engage in higher order thinking and learning.

Differentiated instructional design may be either content general or content specific. A content general design is applicable for many lessons of a common nature while a content specific design is for a specific lesson or unit.

Differentiated Instructional Design

DIFFERENTIATED INSTRUCTIONAL DESIGN MATRIX FOR LITERATURE

	CHARACTER(S)	SETTING	EVENTS	PROBLEM	SOLUTION
LITERAL	**Tell** about the main character, telling how he/she looks and acts.	**Identify** where the story takes place.	**Outline** the events in the story.	**Recall and tell** about the main problem in this story.	**Tell** about the solution to the problem in this story.
RELATIONAL	**Contrast** the main character in the story to someone you know.	**Compare** another place that is similar to the setting in this story.	**Describe** another story that had similar events.	**Explain** a similar problem in another story or in real life.	**Report** an interview with one of the characters to find out their reaction to the solution.
TRANSFORMATIONAL	**Select** one of the characters and tell why that character is the most likable, bravest, least likable, most troublesome, etc. **(characterization)**	**Change** this setting to where you live and analyze how the story events would change.	a. **Dramatize** the events in the story. b. **Change** one event and tell how this would change the rest of the story.	**Examine** the causes of the problem.	**Select** another possible solution to the problem and rewrite the story.
EXTENSIONAL	a. **Develop** a new adventure to the story involving the same characters. b. **Develop** five questions that you would ask one of the characters in order to understand his/her actions.	a. **Design** a travel brochure telling about the location of the story. b. **Decide** whether or not you would like to live in this setting and give reasons for your response.	What was the most important event in this story? Give reasons for your response. **(Evaluation)**	**Assess** how this problem might impact people other than the characters in the story.	**Develop an argument** to support the actions of the main character in resolving the problem in the story.

Figure 3.6

Content General Design

A content general design contains activities that may apply to more than one lesson or unit. Since the activities are stated in general terms it is possible to use them in more than one learning situation. The Differentiated Instructional Design Matrix for Literature (Figure 3.6) is an example of a content general differentiated plan for fiction reading at any grade level. Some uses of this content general design are discussed below.

1. Discussion guide

During a discussion of a story or novel, the teacher may pose questions such as those in Figure 3.6 to elicit thinking from the literal/concrete to the extensional/abstract. Even in a heterogeneous classroom, all students may be drawn into the discussion through well-structured and strategically asked questions. The astute teacher builds students' confidence with easier questions and gradually challenges students to higher levels of thinking.

2. Written activities

Any one of the differentiated activities presented in the Differentiated Instructional Design Matrix for Literature (Figure 3.6) may be used as an individual or collaborative group project to be completed as a written activity. The teacher may assign the activity or students may be directed to self-select and complete one or more of the given activities. Each of the activities also presents possibilities for cooperative group work.

Content Specific Design

An example of a differentiated instructional design for specific content appears in the Differentiated Instructional Design Matrix for U.S. Civil War (Figure 3.7). In this example, the more general learning standards related to the key events, factors, and impact of the American Civil War are itemized into more specific learning standards related to causes, battles, commerce, international relations, and outcomes. The student activities for each of the specific learning standards range from literal, i.e., listing the major causes leading to the Civil War, to extensional, i.e., developing an argument to support the actions of President Lincoln in bringing the war to an end.

As with the content general design, a content specific design may be used for individual or collaborative group activities. The teacher may assign the activities or students may select the activities they will complete.

 # Differentiated Instructional Design

DIFFERENTIATED INSTRUCTIONAL DESIGN MATRIX FOR U.S. CIVIL WAR

Learning Standard: Know the key events, factors, and impact of the American Civil War

Specific Content / Type of Activity	Know the major causes leading to the Civil War.	Know the major battles of the Civil War.	Know the impact of the Civil War on commerce.	Know about U.S. international relations during the Civil War.	Know the factors that brought the Civil War to an end.
LITERAL	**List** the major causes leading to the Civil War.	**Tell** the major battles fought during the Civil War.	**Identify** three major trade and commerce difficulties during the Civil War.	**Name** the other countries involved in the American Civil War.	**Tell** about three major outcomes of the Civil War.
RELATIONAL	**Explain** the causes of the Civil War from the North's (South's) perspective.	a. **Describe** one Civil War battle including preparation, setting, people, events, and outcome. b. **Compare** one battle won by the North with another won by the South. Tell why it was won and what happened as a result.	**Summarize** the reasons for problems with trade during the Civil War.	**Discuss** how other nations responded to the American Civil War.	Conduct a hypothetical interview with a southern plantation owner (slave, ten-year-old boy, businessman, entertainer, etc.) and **interpret** their views on the outcome of the war.
TRANSFORMATIONAL	**Change or add** a historical event and tell how this might have changed the decision to go to war perspective.	**Dramatize** a trial for one of the Northern generals captured by the South.	Would trade and commerce problems be **similar** in other wars? Give reasons for your response.	Were the causes of the American Civil War **similar** to civil wars in other countries?	Could there have been other solutions to the problems faced by the North and South rather than war? (**analysis**)
EXTENSIONAL	a. **Develop** five questions you would ask President Lincoln regarding the decision to go to war. (A classroom partner will answer the questions.) b. **Prove** that these historical events (causes) justify war.	**Draw or depict** a specific Civil War battlefield showing location, troops, artillery, camps, civilian presence.	a. **Design** a plan for a Northern manufacturer of shoes to sell his goods in the South before and during the war. b. **Justify or prove** why it was legal (or illegal) for Northern manufacturers to sell their goods to the South.	a. **Create** a map showing international involvement in the Civil War. b. Was French support for the South justified? Give reasons (**proof**) for your answer.	a. **Create** a timeline showing the major events of the war and a map of the country after Northern victory. b. Develop an **argument** to support the actions of President Lincoln in bringing the war to an end.

Figure 3.7

Differentiated Instructional Design
A PLANNING GUIDE FOR DIFFERENTIATED INSTRUCTION

The Differentiated Instructional Design Planning Guide is a thinking process approach to guide decision making regarding planning for differentiated instruction. The guide has three sections: (1) Desired Results, (2) Lesson Design, and (3) Evidence of Learning. Each section is divided into three columns. Column one contains a series of questions related to differentiated instruction and learning outcomes, column two contains information and data to facilitate answering the planning questions in column one, and column three contains pertinent notes and comments related to the differentiated instructional design process. A detailed explanation of each section follows.

Section 1

DESIRED RESULTS
What's the rationale?

The first question to answer when planning to differentiate instruction is: Why is there a need to differentiate instruction? Valid reasons should exist for differentiation of activities. Differentiation may not always be a desirable option. When students have similar needs differentiation may not be necessary. When students' diversity contributes to the learning of others, whole class activities may be preferable. Understanding the characteristics of the students in the class helps to form the rationale for using a differentiated instructional design.

A corollary question is: What is the basis for differentiation? That is, how will students be grouped for differentiation—levels of performance, interests, learning styles, or other variables? To maintain a manageable plan, the categories of differentiation should be somewhat limited. Too many categories will produce too many activities that may make management difficult. It is probably best to start with a few activities and increase the number as both teacher and students become comfortable and experienced with this instructional approach.

Constructing the Differentiated Instructional Design

A Differentiated Instructional Design Matrix (Figure 3.5) is a framework that organizes and documents the instructional activities. The horizontal axis contains

Differentiated Instructional Design

DESIRED RESULTS

Use these questions as a thinking guide to plan a differentiated instructional design.

PLANNING QUESTIONS AND DECISIONS	INFORMATION AND DATA SOURCES	NOTES AND COMMENTS
1. Why is there a need to differentiate instruction?	Review student data, performance, observations, and professional literature.	The decision and subsequent planning for differentiated instruction may be before a unit of study or any time during a unit of study when it becomes apparent that differentiation is needed to accommodate student needs.
2. How will students will be grouped for differentiation (levels of performance, interests, learning styles)?	Student data on performance levels, interests, or learning styles may be used to determine instructional activity groups.	An informal student interest survey, observational checklist, or pretest may supply additional data.
3. What are the learning standards to be achieved?	Review content, skills, process, and concept standards required at district and state levels.	Select those standards that will be made more meaningful through differentiation.
4. How will learning standards be organized and documented?	A Differentiated Instructional Design Matrix (Figure 3.5) is used to plan and keep track of differentiated activities.	Once the learning standards and the basis for differentiation are decided, a Differentiated Instructional Design is developed. Specific activities will be added later. This plan documents the standards, activities, and categories of differentiation.
5. How will the learning standards be assessed? Are combined or embedded assessments feasible? What assessment materials are available and what materials need to be developed?	Review: a. required and optional assessments b. rubrics and assessments in district curriculum guides, teacher manuals, other sources	Planning for assessment is a recursive process. Assessment strategies and tools are tentatively outlined in the initial stages of instructional design, reconsidered and modified as the design emerges, and then finalized with the finalized product. Students are held responsible for the learning inherent in the activities they performed.
6. How will students' difficulties be recognized along the way?	Use formative assessments and observational techniques to determine students progress or difficulties.	
7. How will assessment results be communicated to students and parents?	Consider report cards, grading scale, portfolios, and other means.	Determine what students and parents need to know before, during, and after the unit of instruction.

tains the learning standards; the vertical axis contains the basis for differentiation. For example, if differentiation is to occur based on cognitive levels, these levels become part of the vertical axis. If differentiation is to occur based on Gardner's eight intelligences, the intelligences become the vertical axis. A specific, well-planned design makes implementation manageable and efficient.

Think About Assessment Strategies

Students' learning may be assessed through a rubric for each of the instructional activities on the matrix. These are performance-based assessments that are embedded in instruction. As with all performance-based assessments, rubrics communicate expectations and define criteria for performance. A selected response assessment is also possible and may be considered especially for the literal types of activities.

Section 1

DESIRED RESULTS – DIFFERENTIATED
Planning Questions and Decisions

Grade 8 Language Arts Class

1. Why is there a need to differentiate instruction?
My students exhibit a wide range of reading abilities. I would like to find some way to meet their needs yet still have them participate as a whole group. I have tried in class ability grouping using different textbooks and was not pleased with it. Students were too segregated. I would like to give them reading assignments on the same general topic but allow them to read material at their level. I could then have them discuss books around a common theme.

2. How will students be grouped for differentiation (levels of performance, interests, learning styles)?
Last year's test results show a wide range of reading abilities. Students will be grouped based on a reading level range. Within each range activities will be selected to tap into more transformational and extensional activities.

3. What are the learning standards to be achieved?
Learning objectives relate to the basic story elements: character, setting, events, problem, solution. I would also like students to make connections to previous readings or information they have related to the story. Activities will be group discussion and one individual writing assignment.

4. How will learning standards be organized and documented?
The Differentiated Instructional Design Matrix will be used to document the various activities for each group based on the story elements.

5. How will the learning concepts be assessed? Are combined or embedded assessments feasible? What assessment materials are available and what materials need to be developed?
The assessment is embedded in the activities. The writing assignment will be scored according to the rubric and incorporated in the student's quarterly grade.

6. How will students' difficulties be recognized along the way?
Students will read independently and meet in their groups to discuss and complete the activities. I will monitor students as they read independently through an informal reading inventory technique to be sure they can handle the material. I will sit in with the groups as they complete the activities and facilitate their work.

7. How will assessment results be communicated to students and parents?
Students will compile their work in a folder. I will complete a rubric on their work. Each student will evaluate their own performance on the rubric. All materials will be sent home to parents.

Differentiated Instructional Design

PLANNING GUIDE—DIFFERENTIATED INSTRUCTION
DESIGN

Use these questions as a thinking guide to plan a differentiated instructional design.

Planning Questions and Decisions	Information and Data Sources	Notes and Comments
1. What are the specific learning standards/benchmarks to be achieved?	Refer to the Differentiated Instructional Design Planning Chart developed in section one.	
2. What are the categories of differentiation?		
3. What activities correlate to each standard and each differentiation category?	Curriculum guides, teaching manuals, professional literature, best practices information, etc. are sources of information for ideas and activities. Use the Differentiated Instructional Design Matrix (Figure 3.5) to document the standards and activities.	In some cases, activities may overlap to such a degree that they are not really different. When this is the case, leave that box on the matrix planning chart blank. It is not necessary to fill in an activity for every box on the matrix.
4. How long will the activities take?	Calendar of school events, holidays, curriculum pacing guides, and testing schedules are sources of information for scheduling.	Develop a specific organized calendar and schedule for the activities. Balance the amount of time with the priority or importance of the activity.
5. What lessons will be taught?	Refer to the Basic Instructional Design described in chapter 1.	Even when most standards are taught through differentiated activities, there may be times when it is appropriate to conduct lessons on common needs with the entire class or with a small group. Each lesson will contain all the components of the Basic Lesson Design. • motivating opening • teaching/learning strategies • materials and resources • grouping • closure • follow up practice • assessment
6. Are there any foreseeable pitfalls in this lesson?		Think ahead to avoid potential difficulties.
7. What will I do if the lesson/unit doesn't work out?		A fall-back plan can keep a flop from becoming a disaster.

Section 2

DESIGN – DIFFERENTIATED
Planning Questions and Decisions
Grade 8 Language Arts Class

1. What are the specific learning standards/benchmarks to be achieved?
The learning standards relate to the basic story components: characters, setting, problem, events, and solution. The Differentiated Instructional Matrix documents the learning standards and how they will be met based on students' reading levels.

2. What are the categories of differentiation?
There are three categories for differentiation: grade level reading ability, above grade level reading ability, and below grade level reading ability. Students will be grouped according to my observations and test scores. If this goes well, I may try to extend the categories based on books that are selected by the students.

3. What activities correlate to each objective and each differentiation category?
Activities will be written out using the terms that correspond to literal, relational, transformational, and extensional learning. Activities will be documented on the Differentiated Instructional Matrix.

4. How long will the activities take?
It is expected that students will do the reading in class and at home and then complete the activities in class over a period of 8 school days. Since this is a "first run," the time period may be adjusted to be more or less than 8 days.

5. What lessons will be taught?
I plan to do a vocabulary introduction activity and a DRTA for the first chapter with group three. This will provide some support and hopefully build confidence for reading the rest of the book on their own.

6. Are there any foreseeable pitfalls in this lesson?
I'll have to monitor students closely since this will be their first experience with group work.

7. What will I do if the lesson/unit doesn't work out?
I could eliminate the group work but it is more likely that I will work through any rough spots and adjust accordingly.

Section 2

LESSON DESIGN

The differentiated instructional design documents and communicates to others what learning standards are being addressed in the classroom. It may be a simple design based on a few learning standards and activities or a more complex design incorporating several standards integrated across content areas. However, the design should never become so complex as to be overwhelming to the students or the teacher. Beginning with a simple design and expanding over the years is an efficient and manageable way to plan.

Differentiated Instructional Design

Section 3

PLANNING GUIDE—**DIFFERENTIATED INSTRUCTION**
EVIDENCE OF LEARNING
Use these questions as a thinking guide to plan a differentiated instructional design.

Planning Questions and Decisions	Information and Data Sources	Notes and Comments
1. How will students demonstrate their learning?	Refer to curriculum resource information and best practices information related to types of assessment.	Refer to your planning notes in section one as decisions regarding assessment are finalized.
2. How will the assessment be scored?		Design appropriate rubrics to show criteria and expectations for performance. Consider student participation in design of rubrics. A differentiated classroom may have common assessments, however, students should be held responsible only for what they have been taught.
3. How will the assessment be reported?	Check schoolwide or districtwide requirements and policies related to grading.	If a schoolwide grading scale is required, be sure to align rubric levels with the grading scale. Consider the development and use of student portfolios as a means of providing feedback to students and parents.
4. How will the assessment results be used?		Use assessment results to determine student strengths and weaknesses and plan the next lessons.

Section 3

EVIDENCE OF LEARNING – DIFFERENTIATED
Planning Questions and Decisions
Grade 8 Language Arts Class

1. How will the students demonstrate their learning?	2. How will the assessment be scored?	3. How will the assessment be reported?	4. How will the assessment results be used?
All students will complete a story map graphic organizer describing the story components.	Story maps will be assessed with a rubric.	Students will receive a copy of the story map rubric scoring results. They will have the opportunity to add to the story map if there are any noted deficiencies.	Assessment results will provide feedback for the students and the teacher regarding comprehension of the story. Scores will be included in the student's quarterly grade report for language arts.
Students will self-select three activities to complete from the Differentiated Instructional Design Activity Organizer. Each selected activity must be from a different row.	The students' written responses will not be scored but will be used in a compare/contrast group discussion of the books.	Students will be assessed on the degree of participation in discussion – none, limited, and involved.	The degree of participation will provide feedback for the student and the teacher on how ideas are communicated.
One of the self-selected activities will be submitted as a written assignment.	Written assignments will be assessed with the appropriate rubric – narrative, descriptive/expository, or persuasive. Students will determine which rubric is to be used according to what type of writing they did.	Copy of the rubric will be returned to the student with the teacher's scoring and comments. Students will be asked to use the rubric to self-score their writing.	Copies of the teacher's scores and the student's scores will be sent home to parents. The teacher's scores will be included in the student's quarterly grade report for language arts.

Section 3

EVIDENCE OF LEARNING

Initially, assessment is considered in section one of the Differentiated Instructional Design Planning Guide. As the differentiated instructional plan nears completion, the assessment of student learning and expectations for performance are finalized and rubrics that define criteria and performance levels are developed.

Differentiated Instructional Design

USING THE DIFFERENTIATED INSTRUCTIONAL DESIGN PLANNING GUIDE

The Differentiated Instructional Design Planning Guide is a thinking process approach to planning. Preservice teachers and new teachers will find it helpful to follow the all the steps in using the model. Experienced teachers with an understanding of instructional design may find that they need only review the questions and activities and focus on those areas that will enhance their planning efforts. This structure is a helpful planning tool, but experienced teachers know that change options and flexibility for improvisation as the plan unfolds are also important.

1. Read the planning guide in its entirety.

Become thoroughly familiar with the planning guide before you begin using it. This will save you time in the long run. Get the "big picture" in mind before filling in the details.

2. Think it through.

Begin with Section 1: Desired Results. Think about the questions in column one and write down your thoughts and reactions. Consult the data and information sources suggested in column two and note the reminders and supplemental information in column three. Add notes and comments of your own that will be helpful in subsequent planning. Planning questions may be deleted or added to fit your situation. Continue through Section 2: Lesson Design and Section 3: Evidence of Learning.

3. Synthesize the information.

The thinking process in step two above provides a great deal of information. Any of the instructional activities may be taught as mini-lessons within the differentiated plan. Section 2 of the Differentiated Instructional Design Planning Guide shows where direct lessons fit into the overall scheme. These direct lessons follow the same format as the Essential Instructional

Design discussed in chapter one. An example of how this plan was used by an eighth-grade language arts teacher appears on page 99.

SUMMARY OF GENERAL PLANNING STEPS FOR DIFFERENTIATED INSTRUCTION

The Differentiated Instructional Design Planning Guide contains the detailed description of how to plan for differentiated instruction. The steps below are a general outline of the process.

1. Think through the process of differentiated instruction using the Differentiated Instructional Planning Guide.
2. Determine the rationale for using a differentiated instructional approach.
3. Determine categories for differentiation. Fill in categories on the Differentiated Instructional Design Matrix (Figure 3.5).
4. Determine what learning standards will be addressed. Fill in learning standards on the Differentiated Instructional Design Matrix (Figure 3.5).
5. Develop activities based on category for differentiation and learning standard. Fill in activities on the Differentiated Instructional Design Matrix (Figure 3.5).
6. Develop mini-lessons as needed (chapter 1, Figure 1.12).

REFLECTIVE PRACTICE

Merely following an outline or filling in a template is not sufficient to develop skill in instructional design. Instructional design is a metacognitive, reflective process where the teacher thinks, reflects, adjusts, redirects, fiddles, and fine-tunes the various components until a powerful lesson plan emerges. When reflection is an intrinsic part of the instructional planning

process and teachers take time to analyze their planning efforts, they learn through their experiences, and future planning becomes more effective and efficient. What Costa (1991) called "inner dialogue" is essential to professional growth, change, and improvement. With experience, teachers feel comfortable taking some shortcuts and understand why and how they are able to do so. It is the "inner dialogue" that Costa (1991) describes that contributes to professional growth, change, and improvement.

Use the Inner Dialogue page that follows to reflect on planning actions, attempts, and results of using the Differentiated Instructional Design. Be open-minded but skeptical. Consider pros and cons, benefits, and challenges. Look beyond what was accomplished to why and how it was accomplished.

INNER DIALOGUE

Take time to reflect on the process you have gone through to plan differentiated instruction. Keep in mind that you are developing planning skills that will become stronger with experience and practice. As with all learning, reflecting on your experience will deepen your understanding. At some point, you will feel comfortable taking some short cuts and you will understand why and how you are able to do so. Keep your notes and refer to them when you plan again.

Fact This is what I did in the planning process.	**React** This is what I think about it and how I might change or modify it.
Some new learning	
Some benefits	
Some challenges	

Differentiated Instructional Design

Monday 10/2	Tuesday 10/3	Wednesday 10/4		Thursday 10/5	Friday 10/6	Notes
8:15—9:05 Assign. E-pen pals Silent Reading	Group Presentations Assign. H.W.	Group Present- ations		8:15—9:05 Use attentive listening w/read aloud (SSR)	State testing	Schedule Conferences
9:10—10:00 Organize Coop groups	Specials Math committee meeting	Graph results of survey (pictograph)		9:10—10:00 Specials- P.E.		
10:05—10:55 Guest panel for PBL examination Assign. H.W.	Guest panel for PBL examination Assign. H.W.	Role play Group 1—Sc. 1 Group 2—Sc. 2	L U N C H	10:05—10:55 E-pen pal reports (SSR)		
11:00—11:50 Supervision				11:00—11:50 Supervision		
11:55—12:45 Specials	Class disc- conflict and feelings in lit. Assign. H.W.	Specials		11:55—12:45 • Collage •move to assigned centers (SSR)	Specials	
12:50—1:40 Staff meeting Assign. Proj. for next mo.	Lab time Use Internet sources	Bringing snapshots to explain scientific process		12:50—1:40 Turn in community survey materials (SSR)	State testing	
1:40—2:35 Group Presentations	Begin to formulate/create mobiles Assign. H.W.	Cont. wk on mobiles—Each group Give prog. report		1:40—2:35 Re-group/move seats (SSR)		

Differentiated Instructional Design

DIFFERENTIATED INSTRUCTIONAL DESIGN PLANNING CHART

Learning Standard(s) and Bookmarks

Categories of Differentiation

Section 1

DESIRED RESULTS – DIFFERENTIATED
Planning Questions and Decisions

1. Why is there a need to differentiate instruction?

2. How will students will be grouped for differentiation (levels of performance, interests, learning styles)?

3. What are the learning standards to be achieved?

4. How will learning standards be organized and documented?

5. How will the learning standards be assessed?

Are combined or embedded assessments feasible? What assessment materials are available and what materials need to be developed?

6. How will students' difficulties be recognized along the way?

7. How will assessment results be communicated to students and parents?

Differentiated Instructional Design

Section 2

DESIGN – DIFFERENTIATED
Planning Questions and Decisions

1. What are the specific learning standards/benchmarks to be achieved?

2. What are the categories of differentiation?

3. What activities correlate to each standard and each differentiation category?

4. How long will the activities take?

5. What lessons will be taught?

6. Are there any foreseeable pitfalls in this lesson?

7. What will I do if the lesson/unit doesn't work out?

Section 3

EVIDENCE OF LEARNING – DIFFERENTIATED INSTRUCTION
Planning Questions and Decisions

1. How will students demonstrate their learning?

2. How will the assessment be scored?

3. How will the assessment be reported?

4. How will the assessment results be used?

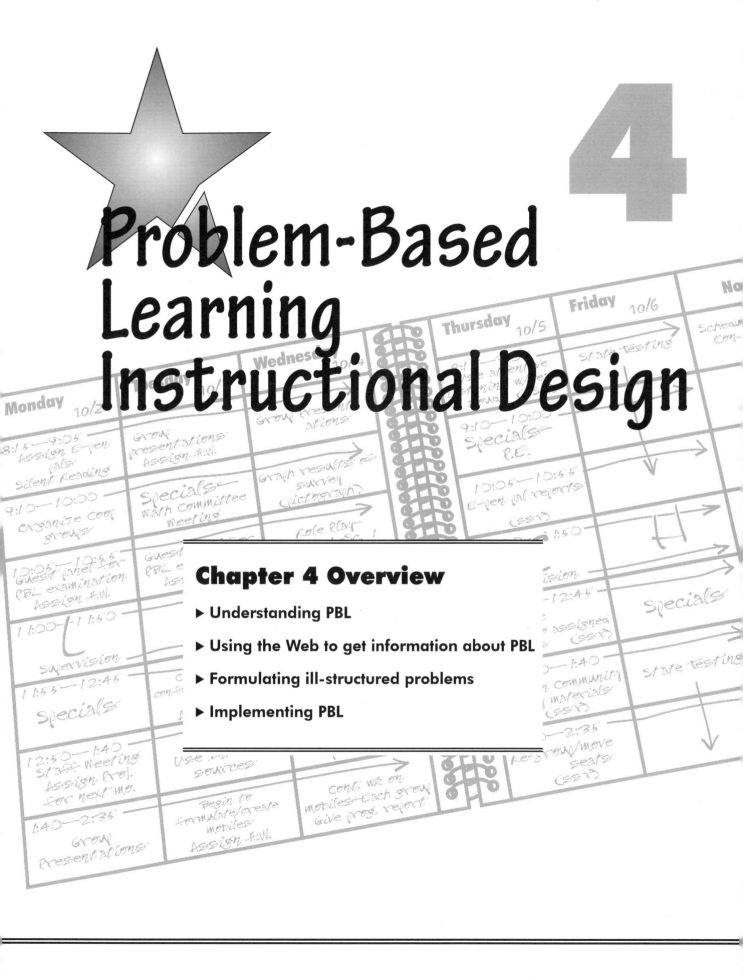

Problem-Based Learning Instructional Design

4

Chapter 4 Overview

▶ **Understanding PBL**

▶ **Using the Web to get information about PBL**

▶ **Formulating ill-structured problems**

▶ **Implementing PBL**

Problem-Based Learning Design

Problem-based learning has roots in the philosophy of Dewey (1913) and the theory of constructivism (Brooks and Brooks 1993). According to Nagel (1999) problem-based learning is student centered, inquiry oriented, curriculum integrated, and collaborative. It begins with an "ill-structured" problem springboard where students are given minimal guidelines and information to begin. They must discuss and specifically define the problem, and then, using a process much like the scientific method, work through to a solution or conclusion. Problem-based learning is touted as "authentic as it gets" (Stepien 1993).

There are no problems . . . only opportunities.
—unknown

Problem-based learning (PBL) was developed at the McMaster University School of Medicine in Canada during the 1960s by Dr. Howard Barrow. In the United States, several medical schools including Harvard University's School of Medicine adopted a PBL model as an alternative to the traditional lecture dominated approach to learning. Problem-based learning is finding acceptance at other levels of education as well, as teachers become convinced of its effectiveness and acquire expertise in using it as an instructional strategy (Aspy, Aspy, and Quinby 1993; Delisle 1997).

Project-based learning is very similar in intent and design to problem-based learning. As presented here, the purposes and procedures for problem-based learning also apply to project-based learning. The Buck Institute for Education offers information and examples of project-based learning on their Web site (www.bie.org).

PROBLEM-BASED LEARNING EXAMINED

Problem-based learning is an approach that capitalizes on students' interest in real-life problems. It is a "process" approach rather than a "content" approach. Students acquire content information and knowledge by using processes such as exploration, research, and collaboration. Students learn to formulate a problem statement, develop action plans, conduct information

SkyLight Professional Development

searches, use data, find and use resources, work collaboratively with others both within the school and outside the school, arrive at conclusions, and communicate findings to others.

Students as early as second grade can successfully participate in problem-based learning (Checkley 1997). Exposure to the problem-

PROBLEM-BASED LEARNING AND CONSTRUCTIVISM WEB SITES

———

http://www.sedl.org/scimath/compass/v01n03/

http://hale.pepperdine.edu/~rsaldric/construct.html

http://carbon.cudenver.edu/~mryder/itc_data/constructivism.html

Figure 4.1

based process at an early age helps students to develop the attitude that learning is the search for information to resolve problems (see Figure 4.1).

Theories of constructivism support learning approaches that enable students to engage in activities in which they make sense of ideas and connect new information and concepts to what they already know. The theories of both John Dewey and Jean Piaget point to the importance of engagement in meaningful learning activities. John Dewey believed that students construct knowledge through experiences that are meaningful to them. He also believed that these experiences must occur in social situations where students work together. Jean Piaget believed that discovery leads to constructing knowledge and is fundamental to learning at each stage of development (Brooks and Brooks 1993).

Constructivist theory fits with brain-based theories that describe learning as connecting new information and concepts to what is already known (Caine and Caine 1991, Jensen 2000). New learning must be fitted into what is already established to be meaningful and lasting.

Those who believe in the effectiveness of problem-based learning as an instructional approach point to the overloaded curriculum and vast amount of information students are required to learn. The traditional lecture, study, test procedure has created bored, uninterested students who seem poorly equipped to solve problems and take responsibility for their own learning. To them school has little relevance to the real world. Problem-based learning

Problem-Based Learning Design

activities that engage students in interesting ways can increase motivation and desire to learn.

THE ROLE OF LEARNING STANDARDS IN A PBL CLASSROOM

Problem-based learning by its very nature integrates learning standards, but the standards involved in the PBL activity may not be completely known initially. As the problem unfolds and students work toward its solution the associated learning standards may change. Effective planning for problem-based learning requires teachers to have in-depth knowledge of the learning standards—to recognize where they occur in the problem activity and ensure they are assessed in some manner. This is not to say that the teacher does no preliminary planning. In planning for problem-based learning, the teacher begins with some learning standards in mind but must be willing to add or delete standards as the problem unfolds and the activity is underway. This requires a highly organized, astute teacher who is able observe students as they plan and note the important learning standards they will address in their study. In addition, the teacher must be able to pull together resources in short order, plan lessons (sometimes on the spot), and constantly think ahead to where the students may lead. The teacher must have a high level of ambiguity tolerance—the ability to work with a degree of vagueness and uncertainty. The Problem-Based Learning Standards Overview (Figure 4.2) is used to document and keep track of the learning standards involved in the study of a particular problem. The standards overview form is a flexible document. It is adjusted as the teacher notes the changes in the direction students take in their problem solving.

Problem-Based Learning Standards Overview

The Problem

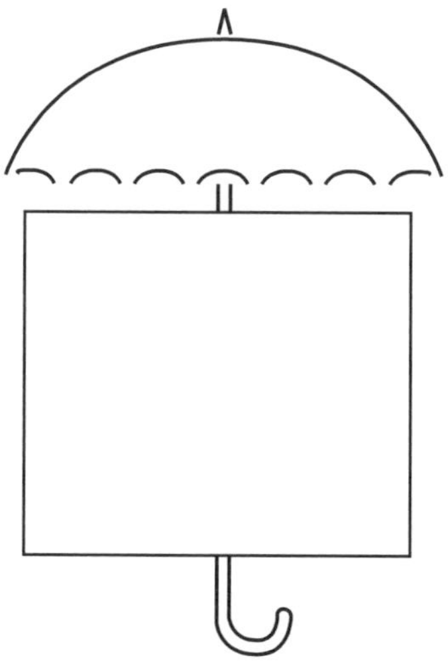

Reading Standards/Benchmarks
1.
2.
3.

Writing Standards/Benchmarks
1.
2.
3.

Listening/Speaking Standards/Benchmarks
1.
2.
3.

Science Standards/Benchmarks
1.
2.
3.

Physical Education Standards/Benchmarks
1.
2.
3.

Social Studies Standards/Benchmarks
1.
2.
3.

Fine Arts Standards/Benchmarks
1.
2.
3.

Mathematics Standards/Benchmarks
1.
2.
3.

Figure 4.2

Problem-Based Learning Design

PLANNING FOR PBL

The Ill-Structured Problem

Problem-based learning begins with an "ill-structured" problem that gives students just enough information to entice them to begin discussion and make connections to previous learning. The Problem-Based Learning Initiative at Southern Illinois University describes a problem as a "goal where the correct path to its solution is not known" (www.pbli.org). The problem deals with some real-life issue of interest to the students. If the goal of education is to prepare students to be able to solve real-life problems, then ill-structured problems are the most authentic (Checkley 1997). In real life, rarely is all necessary information readily apparent when one encounters a problem. And rarely does a real-life problem have only one right solution. It is the task of the students to examine and further define the problem and construct a hypothesis statement. Topics for problem-based learning activities come from real-life issues and problems (Figure 4.3).

TOPICS FOR PROBLEM-BASED LEARNING ACTIVITIES

- Destruction of the rain forest
- Pollution of a local river
- Living in a space station
- Use of fertilizer on suburban lawns
- Migration of the Canada goose
- Bringing the Internet to everyone
- Building a new expressway
- Free medical care for everyone
- Allowing pets in public places
- Year-round schools

Figure 4.3

SkyLight Professional Development

Delisle (1997) says that an ill-structured problem should be developmentally appropriate, grounded in student experience, curriculum based, and allow for a variety of teaching and learning strategies and styles.

According to Stepien, Gallagher, and Workman (1993):

1. Students will need more information than what is initially presented. This helps them to understand more fully what is needed for a solution.

2. There are no right or wrong ways to study a problem. The process depends on the problem itself and the questions generated as the focus for the study.

3. The problem itself may change as information is collected.

4. There are no right or wrong solutions.

Some examples of ill-structured problems are shown in Figure 4.4. Many excellent examples of problem-based units are available at www.ncisc.org.

EXAMPLES OF ILL-STRUCTURED PROBLEMS

Primary Level
Second-grade students would like to keep an alligator as a classroom pet in a school where pets are not allowed. You have been asked to persuade the principal that it is a good idea.

Intermediate Level
The classroom software collection does not cover all the interests of the students in the class. Determine a plan to remedy the situation.

Middle School
Some students are complaining about the food in the student cafeteria. There is a general feeling that the food is tasteless and high in calories. Is this complaint well founded? How may it be remedied?

High School
The mayor has announced a $3 million project to improve the parks and playgrounds in the city. As a member of the committee to make recommendations, how would you go about doing so and what would your recommendations be?

Figure 4.4

Next Steps

When the problem is defined, students plan a course of action and determine how they will go about reaching a solution. Their actions may involve study, research, interviews, and data collection using a variety of resources. Students hone their reasoning and logical thinking through participating in realistic and relevant problem-solving activities. The process is iterative in that as new information is acquired, the problem statement may be altered

Problem-Based Learning Design

and the course of action changed (Checkley 1997). During this stage, the teacher facilitates student discussion and actions. Traditional lesson plans do not fit problem-based lessons; however, the teacher should keep a record of information related to what students do as they pursue the solution to the problem. Students may also be asked to keep a journal or log of their daily activities.

In a problem-based learning setting, students explore beyond the walls of the classroom to collect data that contributes to the solution of the problem. The problem itself is most often related to issues and events of the larger community. The process of learning through problem solving involves coming to terms with what is known or believed and fitting this with new information. New information may conflict with existing perspectives, ideas, and attitudes. Reconciling the new and the old becomes part of the learning process.

EFFECTIVELY LEADING PBL

Problem-based learning is student centered. Students take the lead in planning, directing, and completing their work. They choose resources and evaluate their progress. Several strategies to facilitate problem-based learning are described below.

Cooperative Learning and PBL

Participating in groups enables students to learn with and from one another as they collaborate, discuss, and debate. They strengthen their problem-solving capabilities as they learn to evaluate the accuracy of information from various sources, and they hone their reasoning abilities. Interdependence creates a setting for social learning where students rely on each other to achieve their goal—to come to some conclusion relative to the problem under study. It is not only the problem's outcome that is of educational importance but also the process of achieving it. It may well be that the quality of the outcome produced is dependent on the successful interaction of the members of the group.

Johnson and Johnson (1984) point out that using cooperation in a group setting is congruent with what students will encounter in the world of work. When there are similarities in the behaviors used in school and the behaviors required in the workplace, transfer is more likely. Embedded in problem-based learning are processes that can transfer to other problem-solving scenarios (Fogarty, Perkins, and Barell 1992). Of course, assigning students to groups does not guarantee that they will cooperate. Teachers must teach cooperative skills and structure a setting in which cooperation is encouraged and valued (Bellanca and Fogarty 1991).

Tools and Resources for Learning

The success of problem-based learning as an instructional strategy is in part dependent on the teacher's knowledge of the teaching and learning resources that are available. Problem-based learning requires access to current information and comprehensive resources. Students may use the Internet to acquire information, communicate with field experts, keep track of data through a database, analyze data through computer charts and graphs, produce Web pages related to their problem, and finally communicate their findings and recommendations on these Web pages.

The Internet can be a valuable tool for students and teachers involved in problem-based learning, but keep in mind that the Net is constantly changing and growing. Sites that are available today may not be later. Finding new sites is part of learning to use the Internet. Most Web sites are multilevel. Some are appropriate for the very young to the most advanced. Here are some "starter sites" for teaching and learning with the Internet.

Problem-Based Learning Design

Language Arts
Resources for Young Writers www.inkspot.com/young
The Children's Literature Web Page www.acs.ucalgary.ca/~dkbrown/general.html
Anne Frank Online www.annefrank.com
Flat Stanley: Creative Writing http://207.125.183.3/jobe/CreativeWrit/Flats1.html
Cyberguides for Literature Instruction http://www.sdcoe.k12.ca.us/score/cyberguide.html
International Reading Association www.ira.org

Mathematics
Interdisciplinary Lesson Plans http://www.crpc.rice.edu/CRPC/Women/
    GirlTECH/Lessons/
Cool Math www.coolmath.com
Math Magic http://forum.swarthmore.edu/mathmagic/what.html
National Council of Teachers of Mathematics www.nctm.org
Mathematical Games, Toys, and Puzzles
    http://sal.cs.uiuc.edu/~jeffe/mathgames.html
The Lost Necklace (math problem solving) http://schoolcentral.com/
    Necklace/vic2.htm

Science
Integrating the Internet into the Science Classroom http://kendaco.telebyte.com:80/
    bilband/Possibilities.html
NASA http://www.nasa.gov/
The Wild Ones (wildlife in danger of extinction) http://www.thewildones.org/
Yuckiest Site on the Internet (cockroaches, beetles, and other insects) http://www.nj.
    com/yucky/
The Thinking Fountain http://www.sci.mus.mn.us/sln/tf/
Ask Dr. Science http://www.drscience.com/
Windows to the Universe http://www.windows.umich.edu/

Social Studies
Abraham Lincoln Online http.//www.netins.net/showcase/creative/lincoln.html
The Great American Web Site http.//www.uncle-sam.com/
Historical Almanack http://www.history.org/almanack.htm
The Virtual Tourist http://www.vtourist.com/
National Council for the Social Studies http://www.ncss.org/home.html
Social Studies School Service http://www.socialstudies.com/who.html
Eyewitness: History Through the Eyes of Those Who Lived It http://www.ibiscom.
    com/index.html
National Geographic Society www.nationalgeographic.com
Smithsonian Education http://si.edu/resources

THE TEACHER'S ROLE IN PBL

In problem-based learning, the teacher allows the students to take the lead. The predominant role of the teacher is that of facilitator and coach, providing resources, asking questions to guide students, and helping them to understand their own thinking as they work through the problem. There is a great deal of ambiguity involved in problem-based learning, and teachers must be knowledgeable and confident in the methodology to be successful (Checkley 1997). The teacher must be an astute observer and listener to understand students' needs and offer assistance, resources, or instruction at the appropriate time. The teacher guides, coaches, and provides instruction as students develop a need for specific information or skills related to their study. For example, if the problem involves a study of the quality of water in a nearby river, the teacher may provide lessons on how to test water for impurities, how to use the Internet to obtain information, and how to structure a report to submit to the local authorities.

Teachers who undertake problem-based learning must have a thorough understanding of the process, knowledge of students' needs, coaching/facilitating/teaching expertise, resource awareness and acquisition, and planning know-how. Because so much of the process is of an "as you go" variety, the teacher is constantly aware of what is happening—on one level thinking and working with the students and on another level thinking about the process itself and his or her role as the planner and facilitator.

How Students "Do" PBL

Each problem-based activity differs in its action plan. However, there is a general structure that students find helpful as they begin to study the problem (see Figure 4.5). Modifications to the structure are made for younger students and for other students who have little experience with the process.

Problem-Based Learning Design

STEPS IN PROBLEM-BASED LEARNING

11 **DEBRIEF THE PROCESS USED TO ARRIVE AT THE SOLUTION.**
This reflective step serves to deepen understanding of learning by discussing both successful and unsuccessful strategies used in solving the problem.

10 **PRESENT THE SOLUTION TO A "REAL" AUDIENCE (THOSE WHO HAVE KNOWLEDGE OF THE PROBLEM AND ARE INTERESTED IN THE SOLUTION).**
This step lends authenticity and importance to the work of the group. Regardless of the outcome, the process and findings are shared and explained.

9 **EVALUATE SOLUTIONS AGAINST THE CRITERIA ESTABLISHED.**
The outcome(s) of the study are compared to the criteria that were established to determine whether the group accomplished what it set out to do.

8 **GENERATE POTENTIAL SOLUTIONS TO THE PROBLEM.**
The study group uses the compiled information to answer the questions incorporated in their study. At this point, potential solutions are discussed. Or, if no solutions are feasible, explanations are given.

7 **GATHER INFORMATION (RESEARCH, TESTING, INTERVIEWS, ETC.).**
Each member of the study team may be assigned to collect different pieces of information, which are then brought back to the group. Analyze and synthesize information and data. Information and data is compiled and put into some usable format—outline, graphs, charts, etc.

6 **DEVELOP THE ACTION PLAN.**
Students outline what they will do and how they will do it. Determining roles and responsibilities of group members is another planning facet.

5 **GENERATE QUESTIONS RELATED TO THE PROBLEM STATEMENT.**
Brainstorming specific questions related to the problem provides further focus for study, research, and data collection.

4 **DEVELOP CRITERIA FOR SUCCESSFUL SOLUTION OF THE PROBLEM.**
Students think about the outcome of their study in terms of expectations for performance. This step also helps to direct their focus in terms of the quality of their endeavor and conclusions.

3 **DEFINE THE PROBLEM STATEMENT (WORKING HYPOTHESIS).**
Students work to craft a statement or question that provides focus and direction for their work.

2 **DISCUSS AND EXPLORE THE PROBLEM.**
Students spend time with the problem, discussing its relevancy and what they currently know about it. They may conduct preliminary research that will enable them to better focus and narrow the problem.

1 **MEET THE PROBLEM.**
Students are presented with an ill-structured problem.

Figure 4.5

Problem-Based Learning Instructional Design
A PLANNING GUIDE FOR PBL

An itemized, step-by-step planning process will not fit all problem-based scenarios. However, a flexible structure is helpful in ensuring that important planning questions are considered. The Problem-Based Learning Instructional Design Planning Guide is a flexible structure to assist teachers in considering the important planning questions in developing a problem-based learning unit of instruction. It is comprised of three sections: (1) Desired Results, (2) Lesson Design, and (3) Evidence of Learning. Each of the three sections has three columns: Planning Questions and Decisions, Planning Resources, and Notes and Comments. The Planning Questions and Decisions column poses a series of questions to guide and stimulate thinking during the planning process. The Planning Resources column lists the types of resources and data sources that will facilitate answering the questions in column one. The Notes and Comments column provides information that will further clarify and assist in answering questions in column one. A detailed explanation of each section follows.

Section 1

DESIRED RESULTS
What's the rationale?

The teacher must have a commitment to problem-based learning that is clearly communicated to all stakeholders. This instructional approach may not be fully understood in terms of its philosophical underpinnings and connection to the curriculum, learning standards, and assessment. Communicating the intents and purposes of problem-based learning helps all stakeholders to understand, accept, and support it.

Problem-Based Learning Design

PLANNING GUIDE—PROBLEM-BASED LEARNING INSTRUCTION
DESIRED RESULTS
Use these questions as a thinking guide to plan a problem-based learning design.

PLANNING QUESTIONS AND DECISIONS	INFORMATION AND DATA SOURCES	NOTES AND COMMENTS
1. What is the advantage in using the PBL approach? Why is this approach being selected?		
2. What "problem" topic will become the basis for this learning activity?	Surveys and observations of students regarding interests and concerns in current real-world problems are sources of information for determining a topic for the problem.	
3. What "ill-structured" problem will be stated?		The ill-structured problem contains just enough information to elicit interest and motivation to further define the problem. The problem should have relevance to the students and be motivating. It should present some but not all information necessary to begin the study. Students must add to the information they are given so they have a firm grasp of the problem and what they must do to solve it.
4. What learning standards are likely to be addressed through this project?	Review district and state standards. See Problem-Based Learning Standards Overview (Figure 4.2).	It is not possible to know exactly which learning standards will be involved in the problem-based learning activity at this point, however, they should have some tentative connections in mind.
5. What form of assessment might fit the project?	Review district and state assessments, rubrics for performance, past practices. (See Problem-Based Learning Assessment Planner Figure 4.6).	It is not possible to know exactly which assessments are needed since the learning standards have not yet been finalized. However, think ahead and keep in mind some probable strategies. These will be reconsidered as the problem-based activity progresses.
6. How will students' difficulties be recognized along the way?	Use formative assessments and observational techniques to determine student progress or difficulties.	Use assessment data to plan "just in time" lessons.
7. How will I communicate assessment results to students and parents?		Determine what students and parents need to know before, during, and after the problem-based activity.

Section 1

DESIRED RESULTS – PROBLEM-BASED LEARNING
Planning Questions and Decisions

Grade 10 American History Class

1. What is the advantage in using the PBL approach? Why is this approach being selected?

I've been a teacher for sixteen years. I've seen programs come and go. I haven't changed my teaching much but lately I've realized my students are becoming more complacent and disinterested than ever before. I did some reading on problem-based learning and I think there may be something to it. I'm ready to try something new. I'd like my students to get more involved and interested. (I guess I'd like the same thing for myself.) My rationale for using problem-based learning is that it fits with constructivist theory and brain-based learning. It has been used in other schools with a high degree of success. There's at least enough to support it to allow for a "pilot."

2. What "problem" topic will become the basis for this learning activity?

The topic will be roots and origins of racial discrimination. (Students will work in groups of five—each group will work on the same problem. At the conclusion of the project, we will compare and contrast the actions and reports generated by each of the groups.)

3. What "ill-structured" problem will be stated?

"Three young men of color are walking down a street late at night. One of the young men is in a particularly bad mood because his girlfriend broke up with him that morning. He had no idea how bad things were between them, and now he's in no mood to take harassment when his friends meet him after his night shift at a local restaurant. When the white police officers who stop the young men make a racial comment, the young man responds in kind. The result is a night spent in the police station, and very worried mothers for at least two of the young men."
Adapted from Kobrin, Abbott, Ellinwood, and Horton (1993).

When the story breaks in the morning news, the mayor resolves an investigation. You are placed on the mayor's task force to get as much information on the incident, probable causes, and recommended solutions. How will you go about your task? What information do you need? Who will be most helpful to you? How will you go about formulating your solutions? Your written report to the mayor must be submitted in three weeks.

4. What learning standards are likely to be addressed through this project?

    a. Identify the problem and structure a problem statement.
    b. Develop an action plan. (Individuals will volunteer or be assigned to complete various tasks.)
    c. Formulate criteria for assessing the degree of success of the task force outcomes.
    d. Collect data.
    e. Research legislation related to racial discrimination.
    f. Analyze data.
    g. Assess accuracy of information (data).
    h. Draw conclusions (formulate solutions).
    i. Write a report.

5. What form of assessment might fit the project?

The assessment of student learning will be related to two major aspects of the project: the criteria developed by the students to determine the degree of success of the task force outcomes and the written report submitted to the mayor at the end of the project. An individual assessment will be through the work the student has completed in his/her file.

6. How will students' difficulties be recognized along the way?

I will work with each of the groups and observe the participation of individual students and their progress.

7. How will I communicate assessment results to students and parents?

Students will keep a "file" of their work on the task force. The file will be submitted at the end of the project along with a copy of the written report.

Problem-Based Learning Design

What's the Problem?

The basis for problem-based learning is a problem. The learning standards are inherent in the problem. Assessments are aligned to the learning standards and thus to the problem itself. The problem must be well selected, that is, it should be relevant to students and at the same time hold the potential for important learnings.

Think Ahead

Once the ill-structured problem is designed, the teacher thinks ahead to the potential learning standards and assessments that eventually may become part of the overall design. A flexible mind-set is necessary, since the problem may be altered by the students, thereby changing the learning standards.

Section 2

LESSON DESIGN

The problem-based design is not so much a plan as a preliminary investigation by the teacher—a brainstorming of potential and probable ideas that may be translated into actions as students progress in their problem-based study.

Section 3

EVIDENCE OF LEARNING

Assessment of student learning is part of any instructional approach. In a problem-based learning approach, the assessment is most likely to be performance based and related to the problem solutions or outcomes. A rubric designed for this purpose communicates to students and parents the expectations for performance. The Problem-Based Learning Assessment Planner (Figure 4.6) is used to document the standards and the manner in which they are assessed.

PROBLEM-BASED LEARNING ASSESSMENT PLANNER

Standards Assessed

Assessment Description

Student Directions

Scoring Directions

Materials Needed

Performance Expectations

Figure 4.6

Problem-Based Learning Design

PLANNING GUIDE—PROBLEM-BASED LEARNING INSTRUCTION
DESIGN
Use these questions to plan a problem-based learning design.

Planning Questions and Decisions	Information and Data Sources	Notes and Comments
1. What strategies will students use to further define the problem?		Determine some possible strategies and be ready to prompt students as necessary. Facilitate students exploration of the problem to enable them to verbalize (and visualize) the problem and eventually state a hypothesis.
2. What resources will students need to refine the problem statement?	Check available curriculum materials, software, Internet sites, resource persons.	Identify possible resources and be ready to suggest and recommend them to students.
3. How will students be arranged for this initial exploration?		Determine possible grouping arrangements—or procedures for self selection. Keep track of student groups.
4. How much time will be allowed for the initial exploration?	Check the school calendar and other events.	Students should be aware of the time frame and even participate in its development. It may be helpful to schedule work time on a weekly basis.
5. After the problem is refined, what strategies will students use to gather information?		Although students take the lead in what and how they will do something, the teacher needs to be prepared with procedural suggestions, recommendations, and alternatives. Students will require more support especially when this approach is new to them, or the students are very young.
6. Identify the learning standards that are met through the problem-based study.		The nature of problem-based learning makes it difficult if not impossible to connect the problem-based activities to all learning standards before the study is begun. At some point the teacher must analyze the problem-based activity to account for the learning standards and to avoid redundancy. Documentation is an accountability measure.

Continued on page 132

Section 2

DESIGN – PROBLEM-BASED LEARNING
Planning Questions and Decisions
Grade 10 American History Class

1. What strategies will students use to further define the problem?
Students will discuss the initial problem statement; determine what information they have, what they need to determine. They will develop a more precise written statement of the problem. Main strategies will be discussion, brainstorming, categorizing, and condensing.

2. What resources will students need to refine the problem statement?
Students will have access to the Internet for newspaper articles, editorials, legislation, and other related information. They may bring in any information or resources from other sources.

3. How will students be arranged for this initial exploration?
Students will work in groups of five. I will assign groups to attempt a good mix of personalities and cognitive levels.

4. How much time will be allowed for the initial exploration?
Two or three class periods with out of class time to obtain data.

5. After the problem is refined, what strategies will students use to gather information?
I may invite some colleagues to role play the officers, young men, mothers, etc. Students will be able to interview them to get further information on the incident.

6. Identify the learning standards that are met through the problem-based study.
After students begin their study, I will finalize and document the learning objectives that I listed in section one of this plan.

Continued on page 133

Problem-Based Learning Design

Section 2

PLANNING GUIDE—**PROBLEM-BASED LEARNING** INSTRUCTION CONTINUED
DESIGN
Use these questions to plan a problem-based learning design.

Planning Questions and Decisions	Information and Data Sources	Notes and Comments
7. On an ongoing basis, identify student needs related to skills, processes, and information needed to successfully participate in the problem-based activity.	Observation of students as they work and other informal assessments are used to determine needs. Refer to Basic Instructional Design in chapter 1.	Develop lessons on content, skills, and processes as necessary. For each lesson: • Connect the purpose of the lesson to the problem. Students should understand the relevance of the lesson. • Determine how to present the lesson. • Determine what teaching/learning strategies will be most effective. • Determine what materials are needed to enhance learning. • Determine how students will be grouped for the lesson. • Determine a summarizing, reflective activity that once again connects to the problem.
8. How will students gather data and analyze potential solutions?		Be prepared with procedural recommendations for assistance when needed.
9. What are the foreseeable pitfalls?		
10. What alternatives (options) are available if the activity does not work out?		

Section 2

DESIGN – PROBLEM-BASED LEARNING
Planing Questions and Decisions
Grade 10 American History Class

7. On an ongoing basis, identify student needs related to skills, processes, and information needed to successfully participate in the problem-based activity.

Mini-lessons will be developed for: (1) How to develop an action plan, (2) Keeping track of research notes, (3) Legal criteria for racial discrimination, (4) Historical origins of racial discrimination, (5) Report requirements

8. How will students gather data and analyze potential solutions?

Students will work in their groups to discuss data, brainstorm, rationalize, validate, and prioritize solutions. I will work with the groups as they go through this process.

9. What are the foreseeable pitfalls?

Students don't do their part. Lack of understanding of the project and lack of commitment.

10. What alternatives (options) are available if the activity does not work out?

I would go back to a direct teaching model with the class as a whole instead of using the small group structure.

Problem-Based Learning Design

Section 3

PLANNING GUIDE—PROBLEM-BASED LEARNING INSTRUCTION
EVIDENCE OF LEARNING
Use these questions to plan a problem-based learning design.

Planning Questions and Decisions	Information and Data Sources	Notes and Comments
1. How will students demonstrate their learning?		The evidence of learning is both through the process of the study and the presentation of the findings. It represents the learning standards that have been covered in the problem-based study.
2. How will the assessment be scored?	Student action plans will provide information related to activities and possible performance-based assessments.	The problem-based activity fits well with performance-based assessments. Students should be aware of the assessments and the criteria for performance. In most instances they will participate in developing the criteria.
3. How will the assessment be reported?	Review requirements for report cards, grading scales, etc.	Consider use of student portfolios to document work throughout the project. Use rubrics to communicate standards for performance.
4. How will the assessment results be used?		Use assessment results to determine student strengths and weaknesses and plan follow up instruction. Use assessment results to communicate progress to parents and students.

Section 3

EVIDENCE OF LEARNING – PROBLEM-BASED LEARNING
Planning Questions and Decisions
Grade 10 American History Class

1. How will students demonstrate their learning?	2. How will the assessment be scored?	3. How will the assessment be reported?	4. How will the assessment results be used?
Active participation in group activites.	Teacher observation according to rubric (list of requirements and expectations)	Rubric with teacher comments will be given to each students midway through the project and at the end. Final rubric will be placed in the student's individual project file.	Feedback to students and teacher on group participation.
Selected response test on history and origins of racial discrimination.	Scoring key	Papers returned to students to place in their project file.	Feedback to students, teacher, and parents on knowledge related to racial discrimination. Scores will be included in student's quarterly grade.
Written report (group)	Rubric	Teach conference with each group. Return a copy of the group rubric to each student in the group to be placed in their project file.	Feedback to students, teacher, and parents on final project.
Reflection paper to be completed in one class period on: a. The five most important things I learned in this project b. Why they are important c. How my thinking has changed d. How I feel about the project	General completion rubric: Level 1: Limited responses (1 to 4 points) Level 2: Satisfactory responses (5 to 7 points) Level 3: Extensive responses (8 to 10 points)	Papers placed in individual project file.	Provides a summary/conclusion to the project.
Cumulative Assessment based on items above.	Participation 10 pts. Test 20 pts. Group report 10 pts. Reflection 10 pts.	Score sheet will be compiled and returned to students. An average composite score will be calculated.	Feedback on project. Composite scores will be included in the student's final grade.

Problem-Based Learning Design

USING THE PBL INSTRUCTIONAL DESIGN PLANNING GUIDE

The Problem-Based Learning Instructional Design Planning Guide is a thinking process approach to planning instruction. The questions are a guide to specific and precise planning. Even experienced teachers with an understanding of instructional design but limited experience with PBL will find it helpful to review all the steps in the planning guide.

1. Read the model in its entirety

Become thoroughly familiar with the planning guide before using it. This will save time in the long run. Get the "big picture" in mind before filling in the details.

2. Think it through

Begin with Section 1: Desired Results. Think about the questions in column one and write down thoughts and reactions. Questions may be deleted or added to accommodate specific situations. Consult the data and information sources suggested in column two and note the reminders and supplemental information in column three. Continue through Section 2: Lesson Design and Section 3: Evidence of Learning.

3. Synthesize the information

Thinking through the questions on the planning guide yields a great deal of information. Teachers use this information as a touchstone as they implement the problem-based learning unit. Mini-lessons are designed in accordance with student needs and the learning standards that are being addressed. The format for mini-lessons is the Lesson Plan form (chapter 1, Figure 1.12). An example of how this guide was used by a tenth-grade American history teacher appears on page 127.

SUMMARY OF GENERAL PLANNING STEPS FOR PROBLEM-BASED LEARNING

The steps in planning problem-based learning appear to be simple, but do not be misled. It is an ongoing, complex process that depends upon the direction and focus taken by the students. On-the-spot teaching of mini-lessons and the flexibility to change direction are hallmarks of problem-based learning. With this in mind, the planning steps may be summarized as follows:

1. Determine rationale for using the PBL approach.
2. Use the Problem-Based Learning Instructional Design Planning Guide.
3. Develop the ill-structured problem.
4. Determine the learning standards and benchmarks most likely to be addressed in the activity (Figure 4.6).
5. Determine the assessments that will be used (Figure 4.6).
6. Develop mini-lessons (see chapter 1, Figure 1.12).

REFLECTIVE PRACTICE

The importance of one's metacognition throughout the planning and implementation of problem-based learning cannot be overstated. Perhaps in no other approach does the teacher think as much with the students. Being aware of one's own thinking and reasoning is just as important as being aware of the students' thinking and reasoning. Bringing one's thought processes to a conscious level through reflection and inner dialogue facilitates planning and implementation.

Merely following an outline or filling in a template is not sufficient to develop expertise in planning powerful lessons. Planning is a metacognitive, reflective process where the teacher thinks, reflects, adjusts, redirects, fiddles, and fine-tunes the various components until a powerful lesson emerges. When reflection is an intrinsic part of the planning process and

 # Problem-Based Learning Design

teachers take time to analyze their planning efforts, they learn through their experiences and future planning becomes more effective and efficient. What Costa (1991) called "inner dialogue" is essential to professional growth, change, and improvement. Use the Inner Dialogue page that follows to reflect on planning actions, attempts, and results of using the Problem-Based Learning Design. Be open-minded but skeptical. Consider pros and cons, benefits and challenges. Look beyond what was accomplished to why and how it was accomplished.

INNER DIALOGUE

Take time to reflect on the process you have gone through to plan differentiated instruction. Keep in mind that you are developing planning skills that will become stronger with experience and practice. As with all learning, reflecting on your experience will deepen your understanding. At some point, you will feel comfortable taking some short cuts and you will understand why and how you are able to do so. Keep your notes and refer to them when you plan again.

Fact This is what I did in the planning process.	**React** This is what I think about it and how I might change or modify it.
Some new learning	
Some benefits	
Some challenges	

Monday 10/2	Tuesday 10/3	Wednesday 10/4		Thursday 10/5	Friday 10/6	Notes
8:15—9:05 Assign E-pen pals. Silent Reading	Group presentations Assign A.W.	Group presentations		8:15—9:05 Use attentive listening w/read aloud (SSR)	State testing	Schedule Conferences
9:10—10:00 Organize coop groups	Specials- Math committee meeting	Graph results of survey (pictograph)		9:10—10:00 Specials- P.E.		
10:05—10:55 Guest panel for PBL examination Assign A.W.	Guest panel for PBL examination Assign A.W.	Role Play Group 1-Sc. 1 Group 2-Sc. 2		10:05—10:55 E-pen pal reports (SSR)		
11:00—11:50 Supervision				11:00—11:50 Supervision	Specials	
11:55—12:45 Specials	Class disc.- conflict and feelings in lit. Assign A.W.	Specials		11:55—12:45 • Collage • move to assigned centers (SSR)		
12:50—1:40 Staff meeting Assign Proj. for next mo.	Lab time Use Internet sources.	Bridging snapshots to explain scientific process		12:50—1:40 Turn in community survey materials (SSR)	State testing	
1:40—2:35 Group Presentations	Begin to formulate/create mobiles Assign A.W.	Cont. wk on mobiles-Each group Give prog. report		1:40—2:35 Re-group/move seats (SSR)		

 # Problem-Based Learning Design

Section 1

DESIRED RESULTS – PROBLEM-BASED LEARNING
Planing Questions and Decisions

1. What is the advantage of using the PBL approach? Why is this approach being selected?

2. What "problem" topic will become the basis for this learning activity?

3. What "ill-structured" problem will be stated?

4. What learning standards are likely to be addressed through this project?

5. What form of assessment might fit the project?

6. How will students' difficulties be recognized along the way?

Section 2

DESIGN – PROBLEM-BASED LEARNING
Planning Questions and Decisions

1. What strategies will students use to further define the problem?

2. What resources will students need to refine the problem statement?

3. How will students be arranged for this initial exploration?

4. How much time will be allowed for the initial exploration?

5. After the problem is refined, what strategies will students use to gather information?

6. Identify the learning standards that are met through the problem-based study.

 # Problem-Based Learning Design

7. On an ongoing basis, identify student needs related to skills, processes, and information needed to successfully participate in the problem-based activity.

8. How will students gather data and analyze potential solutions?

9. What are the foreseeable pitfalls?

10. What alternatives (options) are available if the activity does not work out?

Section 3

EVIDENCE OF LEARNING – PROBLEM-BASED LEARNING
Planning Questions and Decisions

1. How will students demonstrate their learning?

2. How will the assessment be scored?

3. How will the assessment be reported?

4. How will the assessment results be used?

Problem-Based Learning Design

PROBLEM-BASED LEARNING ASSESSMENT PLANNER

Standards Assessed

Assessment Description

Student Directions

Scoring Directions

Materials Needed

Performance Expectations

Appendix:
Teaching Standards

As important as instructional planning is, it would be a mistake to assume that it is the only component necessary to good teaching. An analysis of what constitutes effective teaching shows the complex interaction of many components. Teaching is far from being a simple process. Recently developed professional teaching standards describe the important components of effective teaching. Professional standards direct teachers' efforts toward the kind of teaching that makes a difference in the classroom (Darling-Hammond 1997). It matters greatly that teachers know and apply the professional standards.

The Interstate New Teacher Assessment and Support Consortium (INTASC), which includes over thirty states and professional organizations, has defined standards for what beginning teachers should know and do as they enter the profession. The National Board for Professional Teaching Standards (NBPTS) has defined standards for advanced, accomplished teaching (www.nbpts.org). These standards are used to evaluate the performance of teachers who apply for National Board certification. Another set of professional standards is the PRAXIS Series: Professional Assessment for Beginning Teachers, which was developed for use by state and local agencies to evaluate teaching performance. This work was expanded into *Enhancing Professional Practice: A Framework for Teaching* by Charlotte Danielson (1996) to include descriptors and levels of teaching performance. Many state boards of education throughout the United States have adopted professional teaching standards that replicate the components contained in the NBPTS, INTASC, and PRAXIS standards.

INTERSTATE NEW TEACHER ASSESSMENT AND SUPPORT CONSORTIUM
The INTASC standards address the full spectrum of effective teaching components, one of which is planning for instruction. There is a clear connection between instructional planning and each of the other INTASC standards. Since *Powerful Lesson Planning Models* is a book about planning, each of the INTASC standards is listed with an explanation of how it relates to instructional planning. While reviewing these explanations, the reader should be mindful that the standards incorporate more than the teacher's act of planning.

Appendix

Standard 1: The teacher understands the central concepts, tools of inquiry, and structure of the disciplines taught; creates learning experiences to make them meaningful to students.

Implications for instructional planning: As the teacher plans instruction, a thorough knowledge of what is to be taught and how it is to be taught is required. The instructional activities that are planned are of interest to the students and correspond directly to the learning outcome that is intended.

Standard 2: The teacher understands how children learn and develop; provides learning opportunities that support their development.

Implications for instructional planning: In an effective instructional design, the learning concepts and the instructional activities are developmentally appropriate for the students. The lesson planned is both challenging and achievable.

Standard 3: The teacher understands how students differ in their approaches to learning; creates instructional opportunities adapted to diverse learners.

Implications for instructional planning: The instructional plan shows diversification of learning activities based on student needs. Standards for learning are consistent, but the manner in which they are achieved may differ. The selected strategies are chosen to capitalize on student interests and strengths to correct deficiencies.

Standard 4: The teacher understands and uses a variety of instructional strategies.

Implications for instructional planning: The instructional plan shows the use of motivating teaching strategies that are based on best practices. A variety of strategies are used to keep students interested and progressing toward intended outcomes.

Standard 5: The teacher creates a learning environment that encourages positive social interaction, active engagement in learning, and self-motivation.

Implications for instructional planning: The activities in the instructional plan support and promote learning through student participation and involvement in an atmosphere of mutual respect.

Standard 6: The teacher uses knowledge of communication techniques to foster active inquiry, collaboration, and supportive interaction.

Implications for instructional planning: The instructional plan includes use of engaged learning and cooperative grouping strategies as appropriate to the learning objectives.

Standard 7: The teacher plans instruction based on knowledge of subject matter, students, the community, and curriculum goals.

Implications for instructional planning: Instruction is designed to teach important concepts, skills, and processes related to the content area or field of study. Instructional plans are developed to provide students with meaningful learning experiences within the classroom and connect to related learning opportunities within the larger community.

Standard 8: The teacher understands and uses formal and informal assessment strategies.

Implications for instructional planning: The instructional plan shows that student learning is diagnosed continually through observation and informal techniques. Periodic formal assessments are used as summative measures. Students are assessed in terms of what they know and can do related to the learning objectives. Plans show that a variety of assessment strategies are used over time. Provision is made for documentation of student progress and communication of results to students and parents.

Standard 9: The teacher reflects on teaching.

Implications for instructional planning: Instructional plans are analyzed, modified, and improved through introspection and self-evaluation.

Standard 10: The teacher fosters relationships with colleagues, parents, and agencies in the larger community.

Implications for instructional planning: Parents and the community know what students are learning and are given opportunities to collaborate and support that learning. Instructional plans are shared and explained to facilitate understanding and support of the educational program.

NATIONAL BOARD FOR PROFESSIONAL TEACHING STANDARDS

While the INTASC standards focus on the core knowledge, skills, and dispositions teachers should develop (National Commission on Teaching and America's Future 1996), the National Board for Professional Teaching Standards focuses on accomplished teaching practices in the classroom. Instructional planning and organization for teaching and learning is inherent in each of the standards. The National Board describes the standards as follows:

1. Teachers are committed to students and their learning.

Appendix

Accomplished teachers are dedicated to making knowledge accessible to all students. They act on the belief that all students can learn. They treat students equitably, recognizing the individual differences that distinguish one student from another and take account of these differences in their practice. They adjust their practice based on observation and knowledge of their students' interests, abilities, skills, knowledge, family circumstances, and peer relationships.

2. Teachers know the subjects they teach and how to teach those subjects to students.

Accomplished teachers have a rich understanding of the subjects(s) they teach and appreciate how knowledge in their subject is created, organized, linked to other disciplines, and applied to real-world settings. While faithfully representing the collective wisdom of our culture and upholding the value of disciplinary knowledge, they also develop the critical and analytical capacities of their students.

Accomplished teachers command specialized knowledge of how to convey and reveal subject matter to students. They are aware of the preconceptions and background knowledge students typically bring to each subject and of strategies and instructional materials that can be of assistance. They understand where difficulties are likely to arise and modify their practice accordingly. Their instructional repertoire allows them to create multiple paths to the subjects they teach, and they are adept at teaching students how to pose and solve their own problems.

3. Teachers are responsible for managing and monitoring students' learning.

Accomplished teachers create, enrich, maintain, and alter instructional settings to capture and sustain the interest of their students and to make the most effective use of time. They also are adept at engaging students and adults to assist their teaching and at enlisting their colleagues' knowledge and expertise to complement their own.

Accomplished teachers command a range of generic instructional techniques, know when each is appropriate, and can implement them as needed. They are aware of ineffectual or damaging practice as they are devoted to elegant practice.

They know how to engage groups of students to ensure a disciplined learning environment, and how to organize instruction to allow the schools' goals for students to be met. They are adept at setting norms for social interaction among students and between students and teachers. They understand how to motivate students to learn and how to maintain their interest even in the face of temporary failure. Accomplished teachers can access the progress of individual students as well as that of the class as a whole. They can employ multiple methods for measuring students' growth and understanding and can clearly explain student performance to parents.

4. Teachers think systematically about their practice and learn from experience.

Accomplished teachers are models of educated persons, exemplifying the virtues they seek to inspire in students—curiosity, tolerance, honesty, fairness, respect for diversity, and appreciation of cultural differences—and the capacities that are prerequisites for intellectual growth: the ability to reason and take multiple perspectives, to be creative and take risks, and to adopt an experimental, problem-solving orientation.

Accomplished teachers draw on their knowledge of human development, subject matter, and instruction, and their understanding of their students to make principled judgments about sound practice. Their decisions are not only grounded in research and professional literature, but also in their experience. They engage in lifelong learning, which they seek to encourage in their students. Striving to strengthen their teaching, accomplished teachers critically examine their practice, seek to expand their repertoire, deepen their knowledge, sharpen their judgment, and adapt their teaching to new finds, ideas, and theories.

5. Teachers are members of communities.

Accomplished teachers contribute to the effectiveness of the school by working collaboratively with other professionals on instructional policy, curriculum development, and staff development. They can evaluate school progress and the allocation of school resources in light of their understanding of state and local educational goals. They are knowledgeable about specialized school and community resources that can be engaged for their students' benefit, and are skilled at employing such resources as needed. Accomplished teachers find ways to work collaboratively and creatively with parents, engaging them productively in the work of the school.

Bibliography

Aspy, D., C. Aspy, and P. Quinby. 1993. What doctors can teach teachers about problem based learning. *Educational Leadership.* 50 (7): 22–24.

Barth, R. 1990. *Improving schools from within.* San Francisco: Jossey-Bass.

Beane, J. A. 1993. Problems and possibilities for an integrative curriculum. In *Integrating the Curricula,* ed. R. Fogarty, 69–83. Arlington Heights, IL: IRI/Skylight Publishing, Inc.

Bellanca, J., and R. Fogarty. 1991. *Blueprints for thinking in the cooperative classroom.* Arlington Heights, IL: SkyLight Training and Publishing, Inc.

Bellanca, J. 1995. *Designing professional development for change: A systematic approach.* Arlington Heights, IL: SkyLight Training and Publishing, Inc.

Bloom, B. 1984. *Taxonomy of educational objectives: Handbook of the cognitive domain.* New York: Longman.

Brooks, J. G., and M. G. Brooks. 1993. *In search of understanding: The case for constructivist classrooms.* Alexandria, VA: Association for Supervision and Curriculum Development.

Brophy, J., and J. Alleman. 1991. *A caveat: Curriculum integration isn't always a good idea.* Educational Leadership. 49(2): 66–70.

Burke, K. 1994. *How to assess authentic learning.* Arlington Heights, IL: SkyLight Training and Publishing, Inc.

———. 1997. *Designing professional portfolios for change.* Arlington Heights, IL: SkyLight Training and Publishing, Inc.

Caine, R., and G. Caine. 1991. *Making connections: Teaching and the human brain.* Alexandria, VA: Association for Supervision and Curriculum Development.

Canady, R., and M. Rettig. 1996. *Models of block scheduling. In Block scheduling: Time to learn.* Arlington Heights, IL: SkyLight Training and Publishing.

Checkley, K. 1997. *Problem-based learning: The search for solutions to life's messy problems.* Curriculum Update. Summer 1997. Alexandria, VA: Association for Supervision and Curriculum Development.

Csikszentmihalyi, M.1990. *Flow: The psychology of optimal experience.* New York: Harper Collins.

Costa, A. 1991. *The school as a home for the mind.* Arlington Heights, IL: IRI/SkyLight Training and Publishing.

Costa, A., and R. Garmston. 1994. *Cognitive coaching: A foundation for renaissance schools.* Norwood, MA: Christopher-Gordon Publishers, Inc.

Cummings, C. 1980. *Teaching makes a difference.* Edmonds, WA: Teaching, Inc.

Danielson, C. 1996. *Enhancing professional practice: A framework for teaching.* Alexandria, VA: Association for Supervision and Curriculum Development.

Darling-Hammond, L. 1997. *The right to learn.* San Francisco: Jossey-Bass, Inc.

Delisle, Robert. 1997. *How to use problem-based learning in the classroom.* Alexandria, VA: Association for Supervision and Curriculum Development.

Bibliography

Dewey, J. 1913. *Interest and effort in education.* Boston: Houghton Miffin.

Diamond, M., and J. Hopson. 1998. *Magic trees of the mind.* N.Y.: Penguin Putnam, Inc.

Drake, S. M. 1993. *Planning integrated curriculum.* Alexandria, VA: Association for Supervision and Curriculum Development.

Ellis, A. K., and J. T. Fouts. 1997. *Research on educational innovations.* Larchmont, NY: Eye on Education.

Fogarty, R. 1991. *How to integrate the curricula.* Arlington Heights, IL: IRI/Skylight Publishing.

———. 1996. *Block scheduling: A collection of articles.* Arlington Heights, IL: SkyLight Training and Publishing.

———. 1997. *Brain compatible classrooms.* Arlington Heights, IL: SkyLight Training and Publishing, Inc. 198

Fogarty, R., D. Perkins, and J. Barell. 1992. *How to teach for transfer.* Arlington Heights, IL: SkyLight Training and Publishing, Inc.

Gehrke, N. J. 1993. Explorations of teachers' development of integrative curriculums. In *Integrating the curricula,* ed. R. Fogarty. Arlington Heights, IL: Skylight Publishing.

Goleman, D. 1995. *Emotional intelligence.* New York: Bantam.

Good, T., and J. Brophy. 1997. *Looking in classrooms.* New York: Addison Wesley Longman.

Goodman, Y., and K. Goodman. 1998. To err is human: Learning about language processes by analyzing miscues. In *Reconsidering a balanced approach to reading,* ed. C. Weaver, 101-126. Urbana, IL: National Council of Teachers of English.

Guthrie, J., and A. McCann. 1997. Characteristics of classrooms that promote motivations and strategies for learning. In *Reading engagement: Motivating readers through integrated instruction,* ed. J. Guthrie and A. Wigfield, 128–148. Newark, DE: International Reading Association.

Hunter, M. 1984. Knowing, teaching, and supervising. In *Using what we know about teaching and learning,* ed. P. Hosford, 169–192. Alexandria, VA: Association for Supervision and Curriculum Development.

Interstate New Teacher Assessment and Support Consortium. 1992. *Model standards for beginning teacher licensing and development: A resource for state dialogue.* Washington, DC: Council of Chief State School Officers. Available: <www.ccsso.org> (2000, March 1)

Jacobs, H. 1991a. On interdisciplinary curriculum: A conversation with Heidi Hayes Jacobs. *Educational Leadership.* 49(2): 24–26.

———. 1991b. Planning for curriculum integration. *Educational Leadership.* 49(2): 27–28.

———. 1997. *Mapping the big picture.* Alexandria, VA: Association for Supervision and Curriculum Development.

Jensen, E. 2000. *Brain based learning.* Del Mar, CA: Turning Point Publishing.

Johnson, D., and R. Johnson. 1984. *Circles of Learning.* Alexandria, VA: Association for Supervision and Curriculum Development.

Korbin, D., E. Abbott, J. Ellinwood, and D. Horton. 1993. Learning history by doing history. *Educational Leadership.* 30(7): 39–41.

Lewis, A. 1993. Getting unstuck: Curriculum as a tool of reform. In *Integrating the Curricula,* ed. R. Fogarty, 49–60. Arlington Heights, IL: IRI/Skylight Publishing, Inc.

Moye, V. 1997. *Conditions that support transfer for change.* Arlington Heights, IL: SkyLight Training and Publishing.

Nagel, N. 1999. *Real problem solving and real learning.* ASCD Classroom Leadership Online. 3(3).

National Board for Professional Teaching Standards. 1997. *What teachers should know and be able to do.* Available: <www.nbpts.org/nbpts/standards/intro.html> (2000, March 1).

National Commission on Teaching and America's Future. 1996. *What matters most: Teaching for America's future.* New York: Teachers College, Columbia University.

Oakes, J. 1988. Tracking: Can schools take a different route? *NEA Today.* 6:41–47.

Relan, A., and R. Kimpston. 1993. Curriculum integration: A critical analysis of practical and conceptual issues. In *Integrating the Curricula,* ed. R. Fogarty, 31–47. Arlington Heights, IL: IRI/Skylight Publishing, Inc.

Rippa, S. A. 1988. *Education in a free society.* New York: Longman.

Samara, J., C. Pedraza, and J. Curry, eds. 1992. *Designing effective middle school units.* Austin, TX: The Curriculum Project.

Samuels, S. J. 1994. Toward a theory of automatic information processing in reading revisited. In *Theoretical models and processes of reading,* 4th edition, eds. R. B. Ruddell, M. R. Ruddell, and H. Singer, 816–937. Newark, DE: International Reading Association.

Seifert, K. L. 1999. *Reflective thinking and professional development.* Boston: Houghton Mifflin.

Shanahan, T. 1997. Reading-writing relationships, thematic units, inquiry learning...in pursuit of effective integrated literacy instruction. *Reading Teacher.* 51(1): 12–19.

Sizer, T. 1992. *Horace's school: redesigning the American high school.* Boston: Houghton Mifflin.

Skowron, J. 1990. Frameworks for reading instruction. *Illinois Reading Council Journal.* 18(1): 15–21.

Slavin, R. 1987. Ability grouping and student achievement in elementary schools: A best evidence synthesis. *Review of Educational Research.* 57: 293–336.

Sparks, D., and S. Hirsh. 1997. *A new vision for staff development.* Arlington, VA: Association for Supervision and Curriculum Development.

Sparks-Langer, G., and A. Colton. 1991. Synthesis of research on teachers' reflective thinking. *Educational Leadership.* 48(6): 37–44.

Sprenger, M. 1999. *Learning and memory: The brain in action.* Alexandria, VA: Association for Supervision and Curriculum Development.

Stepien, W., and S. Gallagher. 1993. Problem-based learning: As authentic as it gets. *Educational Leadership.* 50 (7): 25–28.

Stepien, W., S. Gallagher, and D. Workman. 1993. Problem-based learning for traditional and interdisciplinary classrooms. *Journal for the Education of the Gifted.* 16 (4): 338–357.

Stigler, J. W., and J. Hiebert. 1999. *The teaching gap: Best ideas from the world's teachers for improving education in the classroom.* NY: Free Press.

Sylwester, Robert. 2000a. *A celebration of neurons: An educator's guide to the human brain.* Alexandria, VA: Association for Supervision and Curriculum Development.

———. 2000b. On teaching brains to think: A conversation with Robert Sylwester. *Educational Leadership.* 57(7): 72.

Tomlinson, C. 1999. *The differentiated classroom.* Alexandria, VA: Association for Supervision and Curriculum Development.

Tyler, R. 1949. *Basic principles of curriculum and instruction.* Chicago: University of Chicago Press.

Wellington, B. 1991. The promise of reflective practice. *Educational Leadership.* 48(6): 4–5.

Wiggins, G., and J. McTighe. 1998. *Understanding by design.* Alexandria, VA: Association for Supervision and Curriculum Development.

Withrow, F., H. Long, and G. Marx. 1999. *Preparing schools and school systems for the 21st century.* Arlington, VA: American Association of School Administrators.

Zemelman, S., H. Daniels, and A. Hyde. 1993. *Best practice: New standards for teaching and learning in America's schools.* Portsmouth, NH: Heinemann.

Index

Notes

SkyLight Professional Development

Notes

Notes

Notes

SkyLight

PROFESSIONAL DEVELOPMENT

We Prepare Your Teachers Today
for the Classrooms of Tomorrow

Learn from Our Books and from Our Authors!

Ignite Learning in Your School or District.

SkyLight's team of classroom-experienced consultants can help you foster systemic change for increased student achievement.

Professional development is a process not an event. SkyLight's experienced practitioners drive the creation of our on-site professional development programs, graduate courses, research-based publications, interactive video courses, teacher-friendly training materials, and online resources—call SkyLight Professional Development today.

SkyLight specializes in three professional development areas.

Specialty #

Best Practices

We **model** the best practices that result in improved student performance and guided applications.

Specialty #

Making the Innovations Last

We help set up **support** systems that make innovations part of everyday practice in the long-term systemic improvement of your school or district.

Specialty #

How to Assess the Results

We prepare your school leaders to encourage and **assess** teacher growth, **measure** student achievement, and **evaluate** program success.

Contact the SkyLight team and begin a process toward long-term results.

2626 S. Clearbrook Dr., Arlington Heights, IL 60005
800-348-4474 • 847-290-6600 • FAX 847-290-6609
info@skylightedu.com • www.skylightedu.com